All _out_
Antique Silver
with
International Hallmarks

by Diana Sanders Cinamon

AAA
Publishing

We're _All About Antiques_

Published by AAA Publishing
2601 Del Rosa Ave. Suite 222A
San Bernardino, CA 92404

ISBN: 0-9785168-0-X

Library of Congress Number:
2006903859

Printed in China

Dedicated to:
my husband, Seth and my
mother, Giorgina

Table of Contents

Acknowledgments

Special thanks to:

Prices4antiques.com in Dayton, Ohio for allowing us to reprint images from their web site.

Replacements Limited in Greensboro, North Carolina for allowing us to reprint images from their web site.

Susan O'Neal, Newport Beach, California for allowing us to use photographs from her collection of silver.

Daniel Freund, Studio City, California for allowing us to use photographs from his collection of silver.

Lynette Smith, All My Best Copy Editing in Yorba Linda, California for her assistance, guidance and expertise.

Mischa Dobrotin, Antique Metals Instructor, North Orange County Community College, Anaheim, California, my first metals teacher.

Introduction

After reading this book, you will know more than many of the people in the business.

When I decided to write this book, I wanted to make sure it contained the right kind of information. This book is not a history lesson. Instead, it gives you information to identify the age, quality, and origin of antique silver from many countries.

I have taken what I feel is the most important information for collectors and appraisers and put it in one place. This book will help you:

- Discover the difference between silver items and items that just look like silver.

- Understand what metals are mixed with silver and how they affect silver quality.

- Identify important construction techniques and how they affect quality.

- *Circa date* a piece of silver and identify the maker.

- Know what makes a piece of silver collectible and why.

When I stop at a booth in an antique mall or a flea market, it's because I see something that entices me to take a closer look. I can take a handful of what looks like a pile of junky silverware, lay it on a table, and know which pieces are at least antique and probably unmarked silver. I find those items that have been overlooked by the untrained eye, especially in antique stores.

Right now, you may be saying, "Well, she's an expert. Of course she knows what to look for." But over the years, I have come up with a list of questions that I ask myself.

As a teacher of antique metals and antique jewelry, I have shared these questions with my students to help them figure out what they have. Now I want to share those questions with you and teach *you* to ask the right questions, follow the clues, and get the right answers.

Once you know the questions to ask, you will be able to figure out your item's age, value, and origin. You will be able to tell if there is anything that makes it special, collectible, or rare.

Some time ago, I stopped at a small antique store along the highway to Palm Springs. Inside, the store was packed with antiques, collectibles, and jewelry. As my eyes moved around the room, the sales clerk struck up a conversation with me. He noticed that I was looking more than casually at the jewelry in the glass case. He told me that the owner was a Gemologist and that everything was guaranteed to be exactly as marked. I was a little disappointed, because I felt that all the "good stuff" would be priced for profit.

The sales clerk began pulling out trays full of fine and "costume" jewelry for me to examine. I spent about an hour sifting through trays and trays and bags and boxes of fine and costume jewelry. At one point, I found a Sterling bar pin with this mark:

Since it was just silver, the clerk sold it to me for $10. It was done in the *Arts and Crafts* style of jewelry that was never very popular. Today, though, there is not a lot of it around, making it more valuable. The mark belonged to the Unger Brothers, one of the most prominent jewelers in the early 20th century. My $10 purchase was worth $225. The Gemologist knew gems and metals but knew nothing about antique jewelry. I spent $165 that day and left with about $1,600 worth of antique jewelry that I purchased at *retail*.

This book will help you look at silver and its imitators from a different viewpoint.

You'll have a fun and exciting experience as you ask each question to find a new treasure.

Not only will this book guide you, step-by-step, through the maze of marks, styles, history, and mystique that surrounds silver, but it will help you avoid the biggest mistakes most beginning collectors make.

If you buy one book on silver, this should be it.

Happy Sleuthing!

Chapter 1: Tools of the Trade

Examining Silver

Whether this is your hobby or your profession, you will need some tools. Fortunately, you already have the most important tools you need – your hands, your eyes, and your nose (yes, silver smells different).

When you pick up a piece of silver, notice how it weighs in your hand (its "heft"). I can usually tell just by the weight whether or not the piece is silver or silverplate. Most people are surprised when I tell them that silver is usually *lighter* than silverplate. Later in this book, I will tell you why.

Let your hands feel over the surface. You will notice dents, deep scratches, and large solder repairs with your hands a lot faster that you can find them with your eyes.

You should have a good **10 power fully corrected, triplet loupe.** A triplet simply means that the magnification is accomplished by means of three lenses. Since there can be some distortion at the edges, a *corrected* loupe minimizes that distortion and gives you a larger field of vision. Currently, 20.5mm is the popular size. You can see more. It costs more than most of the bargain brands, but if you have an interest in antiques, you'll find that you will quickly graduate to a professional quality loupe. This one tool will help you in all areas of antique identification.

You can use the loupe to look at the surface of your item. The quality and smoothness of the surface will help you decide how well the item is made. You can also use the loupe to take a closer look at the areas you felt with your hands.

Sometimes, too much of a good thing is not helpful. The same is true with loupes and hallmarks or maker's marks. After decades of polishing, marks can wear to the point that they are barely visible. Sometimes, a 10x loupe is too much. In these cases, you need a **6x** power loupe so that the mark is not magnified beyond the point of recognition. Sometimes, turning the item so that the light reflects off the item from a different direction makes it easier to decipher marks.

Both a 10 power triplet and a 6 power cup loupe are shown in Figure 1-1. The 6 power loupe is perfect for carrying around in your pocket or purse.

The most common mistake people make when using a loupe is how to hold it. You do not hold a loupe several inches away from your eyes like you hold a magnifying glass. Place your index finger through the opening that closes over the loupe. In the photograph, it is the part that says "TRIPLET".

Figure 1-1: 6x loupe and 10x loupe

Rest your thumb on your cheekbone. The loupe should be about 1" from your eye. Bring the item towards your loupe until the item you are trying to look at comes into focus. This is usually about 1" from the loupe. You may need to adjust the distance of your piece, depending on your vision.

If you wear glasses, you can decide whether or not it is more comfortable to use the loupe with or without your glasses. Some people take them off because they are afraid of scratching their glasses. With practice, you can rest the loupe on the lower rim of your glasses or hold it just in front of it. Most importantly, **keep both eyes open when you use your loupe.** You can strain your eyes if you keep one eye closed and look through the loupe with the other.

Silver actually has a smell that is different from other metals. It is a heavy metallic smell. Sometimes it will tingle the way a tart glass of wine affects the sides of your mouth (really). It does not always work for small items, but if you have nothing to test an item with and you can detect a strong metallic smell, it may be worth investigating further.

Next, either a **cloth or metal measuring tape** is useful. Sometimes the value of a piece of flatware changes dramatically because of size, as we will see later when we look at flatware services. Sometimes it is the only way you can tell the difference between two similar pieces by the same manufacturer.

Testing Silver

While silver testing is not recommended for marked items, many American silver pieces from the early to mid 19th century are not marked. In fact, laws regulating the marking of silver with its fineness content were not enacted in the United States until 1906. While most manufacturers marked large silver items in 19th century America, it was by custom and practice, not by law. You may find a **silver-testing solution** helpful. It is available for about $4 per bottle. Proper silver testing will be covered in Chapter 3. If you cannot tell by looking whether a piece is plated, it is best to have some silver-testing solution ready when you need it. Remember, silver testing is not recommended for marked pieces.

Most silver manufacturers thought enough of their work to mark their goods even when not required by law. Most countries have some legal requirements for marking silver, so a good silver-marks book is essential. We have included many of the marks you will find, so you can carry one good book with you and always be prepared.

Weighing Silver

A Riddle: Which weighs more, a pound of feathers or a pound of silver?

Silver is weighed using the troy system, which originated in Troyes, France. There are 12 troy ounces in a troy pound. Here in the United States, when we weigh things like fruits and vegetables, we use *avoirdupois* (avoir.) weight, which has 16 ounces to the avoirdupois pound. One troy ounce is equal to 1.09714 avoir. ounces, so a troy ounce is heavier than an avoir. ounce. Even though the troy ounce is heavier than the avoir. ounce, there are only 12 troy ounces to the troy pound, not 16. Twelve times 1.09714 = 13.165 avoir. ounces. The pound of feathers is heavier. To convert avoir. ounces to troy ounces, multiply by 0.9116.

If you do not have a troy scale, you can use a postal scale (Figure 1-2) to weigh smaller items, as long as you remember to multiply your result by 0.9116.

If you really get serious about being a silver collector, you might want to think about weighing the silver. Some flatware patterns, like Wallace *Grand Baroque,* were heavier before World War II. You should expect to pay more for a pattern that has more silver.

Figure 1-3 shows a scale used for troy ounce measurements. Suspend the scale using the loop at the top, and then hook the item on the other end. Make sure the scale is set to zero. If your piece does not have a handle, try using a rubber band around a small section of the body and then put it on the hook. The postal scale has a 16-ounce capacity (avoir.) and the troy scale has a 10-ounce capacity.

Figure 1-2: Postal Scale

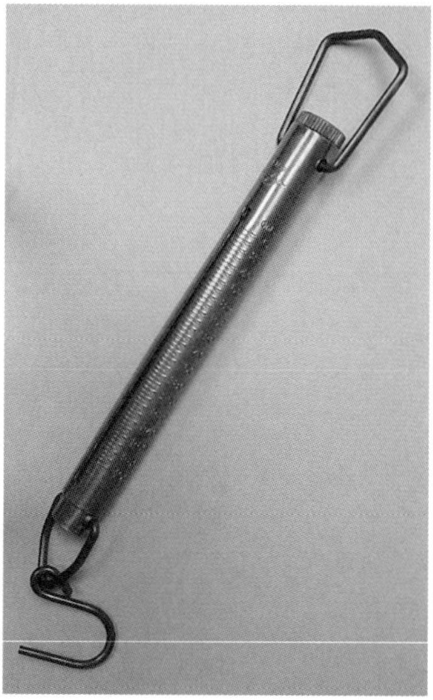

Figure 1-3: Hanging scale for weighing silver

The third picture is a digital scale with 150-gram capacity, or 4.822 troy ounces. This type of scale is used for small jewelry items.

Figure 1-4: Small jewelry scale

To make things a little easier, a chart of weights, measures and conversions is shown in the appendix at the end of the book.

Now that we know the tools we need and how to use them, we are all set to begin our adventure.

Chapter 2: Silver as a Precious Metal

In Chapter 1, we became familiar with the tools we will need to look at silver. Before we decide how old a piece is or who made it, we'll need some background information about silver.

Silver has been thought of as a valuable metal since ancient times. There are references to weighed silver dating to about 2100BC, leading us to believe that someone thought it valuable enough to keep records of its weight.

Figure 2-1: Silver price history

Figure 2-1 shows over six hundred years of silver price history expressed in 1998 dollars. At a high of $806 per ounce, it is easy to understand why various countries of the world made strict laws about silver content.

Silver was probably discovered by accident. When it occurs in nature, silver does not shine. It is an ore with a dull surface and has to be refined. It was probably discovered accidentally, possibly due to a forest fire in an area that was rich with silver ore. It may have caused a natural refining process that made the shiny white metal appear like a glistening pool of silver.

While silver does tarnish, it does not corrode as quickly as metals like iron. Pure silver is very soft. It can be hammered out into sheets so thin that it would take 100,000 sheets to make a stack one-inch high. These sheets are so thin that light shines through them. It was soon discovered that something had to be added to pure silver to give it greater tensile strength; that is, to make it hold its shape. It needed to be stronger and have better wearing quality, too.

Early metal workers learned to combine (alloy) the silver with another metal. Copper turns out to be a good alloy for silver. (Alloy is a noun and a verb.) Adding copper to silver gives the required degree of hardness and makes it more flexible (ductile). A finished piece with more copper can be thinner and it will still have greater tensile strength than a thicker piece with more silver. A spoon made of 100% silver would be too soft to use. It would have very low tensile strength.

Pure copper is red-orange in color, but its addition to silver does not cause a change in the color until the copper content gets close to 50%. The finished piece will still look like pure silver until it reaches this percentage of copper.

Sterling

Since you can add almost 50% copper before you notice a color change, it did not take long to question the amount of alloy used to strengthen silver, since silver was so much more expensive than copper.

The majority of countries that produce silver hollowware and flatware generally use a silver content between .650 *fineness* and .950 *fineness*. Silver *fineness* refers to the amount of actual silver that the piece contains and is most commonly expressed in numbers.

Most countries either have some type of marking rules or some legal requirements for silver content combined with a marking system for silver. Some countries like, Great Britain, have centers in major cities where silver is tested and marked as a guarantee to the consumer that the content meets their content standard of 925 parts silver per 1,000. Sterling silver then, is 0.925 fineness.

Coin Silver

Since there were no silver marking laws in America in the 19th century, American silver manufacturers did not have to use the Sterling standard used by the English silversmiths.

American silver manufactures used "coin" silver to make their items. *Coin silver* was the amount of silver used in American coins, or 900 parts per 1,000. They did this to save money, because they were using less silver and silver was expensive and scarce. There were plenty of coins available; so they melted them down to make silver goods. In practice, coin silver items ranged between .892 and .900 fineness.

Until the time of the American Civil War, most American silversmiths worked in what we call the coin standard. Many silversmiths stamped their finished wares with the words "coin" or "dollar," indicating that the quality was at least that of the American silver dollar.

Tiffany switched to the Sterling standard in 1851; Gorham switched to the Sterling standard in 1868. After the American Civil War, more and more manufacturers began to use Sterling silver (.925) to keep up with changing trends and to compete with English imports.

American Coin Silver Marks

These are some markings that might appear on coin silver:

1. The words "Coin," "Pure," "Pure Coin," "Standard," "Premium," "Dollar," "Dollars," "Quality," "C," "D," all followed by a number indicating the pennyweight. Sometimes just the fineness is shown as in ".900," and "900/1000." These terms were in common use by 1830.

2. Maker's initials or name, sometimes enclosed in a rectangle, oval or a shaped shield, and sometimes including a city name.

3. Pseudo or fake hallmarks that looked like English marks of the period. American silversmiths were in competition with the English and tried to make their marks look like English hallmarks. These pseudo hallmarks could be a lion, an eagle's head, a bell, a star, or a hand. They were used as far back as 1800.

The silver marking laws, which took effect in 1907, allowed manufacturers to stamp the word "coin" on their wares as long as the content was at least .900 fineness. This implies that some silversmiths were still choosing to use a coin standard. **When you see a piece marked with the words "coin" it can still be a twentieth century piece.**

Close or French Plate

The earliest form of plating, called *French* or *close plate*, is believed to date back to the 14th century, although it was not in common use until the 18th century. Items made of iron or polished steel, like knife blades, buckles, and spurs, were first coated with molten tin. Next, multiple layers of pure silver lead were applied. Each silver layer was *burnished*, a process of rubbing the surface with a tool in an attempt to make the surfaced more durable. You have already learned that pure silver is very soft, so the pure silver surface wore away quickly.

Close plating was time-consuming and expensive. Close plate tended to rust because of the base metal underneath, which was usually iron. By the 19th century, close plating was only used to patch and cover exposed "spots" on Old Sheffield. Old Sheffield plate is discussed below. Close plating became obsolete by the end of the 19th century, when more effective methods such as electroplating were in common use.

Mercury or Fire Plating

This method dates back to the 16th century. Powdered gold or silver was mixed with mercury in a small container called a "crucible," and then heated to form a solution called an *amalgam*. After processing the amalgam and then removing as much mercury as possible through a cloth, the final product was a paste. The paste was one-third precious metal and two-thirds mercury. The base-metal body to be plated was first prepared with a solution to aid in bonding. The paste was then applied to the item and fired to burn off the rest of the mercury. This method continued to be used until electroplating was perfected in the mid-19th century.

This process worked best for small items, like buttons. It was a more effective process for gold gilding than for silver gilding. Larger pieces were generally lined using mercury gilding; they were not fully plated. These pieces are very rare today.

Old Sheffield Plate

In 1743, Thomas Boulsolver of Sheffield, England, discovered that he could bind a sheet of Sterling silver to a copper ingot by pressing and rolling the two metals into a workable sheet. The friction from the process caused enough heat to fuse the metals to each other. This sheet could then be made into a teapot, a tray, or other household object. During the late 1760s, the silver was fused to both sides of the copper, making a kind of "silver sandwich." Silver pieces consisting of this sandwiched metal eventually became known as *Old Sheffield plate.*

Figure 2-2 shows a 1904 patent for reducing metal bars to sheet. As heated metal is forced into the rolling mill, the rollers compress, squeezing the metal to the desired thickness. In practice, the ingot is reduced through a series of rolling stands, each one making the metal a little thinner than the previous rolling stand.

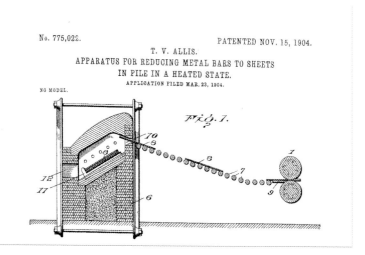

No. 775,022.

PATENTED NOV. 15, 1904.

T. V. ALLIS.

APPARATUS FOR REDUCING METAL BARS TO SHEETS IN PILE IN A HEATED STATE.

APPLICATION FILED MAR. 23, 1904.

NO MODEL.

Fig. 1.

Figure 2-2: 1904 rolling mill patent #775,022

Even though other countries produced Sheffield plate in the 18th century, the English excelled at making Sheffield plate and received over 90% of the orders for it. Therefore, much of the remaining

Sheffield plate will be English.

Identifying Old Sheffield Plate

The undersides of Old Sheffield plate were tinned rather than silver-plated. This means that areas like the underside of a sugar bowl cover or the undersides of candlesticks were covered with tin, not silver. Tinning is done by coating the under-surface with molten tin, and that surface has a slightly rougher look than sheet.

Many pieces of Old Sheffield plate, such as urns and coffeepots, were formed by taking a piece of sheet and rolling it into a cylinder. The cylinder had a seam. Originally, this seam was burnished to hide the seam. After years of polishing, the seam becomes visible. If you breathe on the area, forming a frost, the seam can show up as an orange cast of the copper at the seam line. The presence of an orange seam line, all other things being equal, is proof that the item is Old Sheffield plate.

Since Sheffield plate is a "silver sandwich," the exposed edges have to be rolled over or covered with silver wire or thread (called a wrapped edge) to prevent people from seeing the copper layer in the middle. Look for rolled edges, too.

Sometimes an area like the rim of a teapot or coffeepot, on which the lid rests, is *not* rolled. If you can angle it so you can look at the edge with your loupe, you will be able to see the metal layers with the copper in the middle.

If your piece has a coat of arms engraved on the surface, try breathing around the edges. Sheffield plate manufacturers inserted silver sections so the engraving would not cut through to the orange, copper layer. The air will condense around the outline, giving you an indication that the piece is not solid silver.

Dating Sheffield Plate

1758 – Joseph Hancock of Sheffield, England developed a single-lapped edge which involved rolling the edge over to hide the layered edge. In the early stages of Sheffield plate manufacture, the exposed silver edge was covered with silver solder to hide the two-layered edge. While little Sheffield plate has survived prior to this date, it does give us a dating clue.

1760s – Fused plate was double sided, giving us another dating clue.

1768 – Wire was made from fused plate. It could be used as a wire edging or flattened and applied to the raw edge.

1770s – Fused wire was used to make small wire baskets, bowls and epergnes. Sheffield plating worked very well for these types of pieces and survives in large numbers.

1780s forward – Sheffield plate manufacturers used a method called "flat-chasing," which was a series of short lines or dots that was used to decorate the surface with a design. They used flat chasing because engraving would have pierced the Sterling surface and exposed the copper underneath.

1784 forward – Legislation was introduced in England that allowed manufacturers to use a maker's mark and one device such as a star or a triangle, but the mark could not resemble marks used on silver.

1790 forward – Sheffield plate manufacturers began to insert heavy panels of Sterling silver to the front of pieces so they could meet requests for family crests and shields called "armorials." It was less expensive than making the entire top layer thicker to allow for deep engraving as they did before about 1790. Engraved designs surround the inset Sterling to hide the border where the two substances met. But with close inspection, the lines where shields were inset are visible.

-By 1800 – Sheffield platers were using a thin sheet *of pure silver* that was applied *over the body,* just large enough to allow for engraving. Pure silver tarnishes more quickly than the body made of Sterling (0.925 fineness).

1815 – At the end of the Napoleonic wars there was an influx of poorly made fused plate from France. In response to protests, Sheffield plate manufacturers were allowed to add a crown (the Sheffield town mark) to their wares to help the consumer tell the difference between Sheffield plate and foreign imports.

By the **1820s** – maker's marks often consisted of the full maker's name, although some maker's continued to use initials alone.

Figure 2-3: Sheffield crown town mark

1860s – The demand for fused plate was replaced by a new process called *electroplating*. Expect to see little, if any, fused plate past this time (more about electroplating later on).

Collectible Items Made of Old Sheffield Plate

–By 1774, a wide range of Old Sheffield plate items was being produced, as noted by the *Sheffield Directory* published that year. As a collector, expect to see everything from argyles to writing stands. An *argyle* is a gravy bowl with a hollow wall for hot water that keeps the gravy warm. They are very rare and very collectible.

Figure 2-4: Sheffield plate argyle, early 19th century

The *Sheffield Directory* also lists the following items: bottle labels, bread baskets, bridle bits, buckles, buttons, candlesticks, canisters, castors, cheese toasters, chocolate pots, coffee pots, cream jugs, cream pails, crosses, cruet frames, cups, dish rims, dishes, epergnes, goblets, jugs, knife and fork handles, lamps, lemon strainers, measures, mustard pots, salts, sauce pans, scallop shells, skewers, snuff boxes, snuffer stands, spoons, spurs, stirrups, sugar baskets, tankards, tea kettles, tea pots, tea trays, tea urns, tumblers, tureen ladles, water bottles, water plates, and wine funnels.

Between 1787 and 1815, more forms were added, including asparagus tongs, bread baskets, coasters, communion sets, decanter stands, entré dishes, honey hives, liquor frames, marrow spoons, plate warmers, services, tea bells, toasting forks, tobacco boxes, and wine tasters.

There is something for every collector. If you're brave, try collecting one of each.

Electroplate

In 1840, Elkingtons of Birmingham, England, accomplished a much simpler method of covering a base metal with silver. A completely formed base metal object was suspended in a chemical solution along with solid silver ingots. Electrical current caused silver particles to travel through the solution to the suspended object, where it deposited a layer of pure silver onto all its surfaces.

This electroplating process used a lot less silver than a Sheffield plate "sandwich." It did not require the labor to hide the edges, so it was much less expensive to make.

Figure 2-5: Pen casings being dipped into electroplating tanks

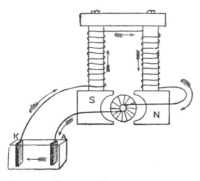

FIG. 12. DYNAMO MACHINE CONNECTED IN SERIES SENDING CURRENT THROUGH PLATING VAT.

Figure 2-6: Diagram of the electroplating process

In 1851, Prince Albert of England organized the first modern, international exposition ever held in the world. It was called the Great Exhibition. It was held at the Crystal Palace in London, England. People came to see the wonderful new products available because of the Industrial Revolution taking place across Europe and in the United States. It was here that many people saw the new invention called electroplating.

Sometime **after** the Great Exhibition of 1851, Old Sheffield plate became obsolete because of this amazing invention. Consequently, Old Sheffield plate is more collectible today.

Electroplating in America

Electroplate manufacturers in England actually set up a program (for a fee) whereby manufacturers could come and learn this patented process. Many American silver manufacturers learned the process of electroplating from Elkingtons in England. John O. Mead, an American Britannia-ware manufacturer, is believed to be the first American to learn the process. After learning this new trade, he returned to America and in 1845 formed a partnership with William and Asa Rogers in Connecticut. This partnership lasted only until 1846. Mead returned to Philadelphia, and the Rogers brothers now knew the process of electroplating. They introduced the *1847 Rogers* line of silverplated flatware. **1847 is the date we usually associate with the beginning of silverplated flatware in America.**

With the development of electroplating, manufacturers no longer had to go to the trouble of hiding edges by rolling them over or covering them with silver wire. On many pieces made of electroplated silver, the edges end abruptly. The plating process covered the edge with silver, hiding the base-metal layer from view.

Aside from the price, silverplate had other advantages over Old Sheffield plate. Old Sheffield plate forms were generally limited to things that could be formed from sheet. Electroplated wares could be made from cast forms that used much more intricate patterns that rose from the surface of the ware.

Some Marks on Electroplated Wares

EP: Electroplate
EPB: Electroplate on brass
EPBM: Electroplate on Britannia Metal
EPC: Electroplate on copper
EPNS: Electroplate on nickel silver
EPNS-WMM: Electroplate on nickel silver with white metal mounts
EPWM: Electroplate on white metal

American Silverplated Flatware Marks

The problem with electroplated silver is that pure silver tarnishes quickly and the silver layer is thin and tends to wear off. Not surprisingly, the American silverplating industry developed internal standards for the thickness of the silver coating on flatware. In practice, 2.5 ounces of silver for a gross of teaspoons was used for *standard plate*. *Double plate* used 5.0 ounces of silver per gross, *triple plate* used 7.5 ounces, and *quadruple plate* used 10.0 ounces of silver per gross of teaspoons. This is not a lot of silver, but it was at least some indication of the durability of the silverplate.

Sectional Plate

In **1868**, Marshall Forbes of the Meriden Britannia Company filed patent number 75,258 (Figure 2-7.) With some parts of utensils, like fork tines, the silver wears off quickly. Since we now know that silver was a very expensive commodity in the 19th century, it was logical that manufactures would develop ways to address wear points without wasting silver. This was done by the *sectional plating* method. This is believed to be the earliest patent filed in America for this process. In their 1877 catalog, the Meriden Britannia Company published an engraving of their patented sectional plating machine which was designed to position pieces so that high wear areas would receive extra silver. Sometimes, the words "sectional plated" or "sectional plating" appear on the back of a piece of silverplate. You can use this as a clue that your piece could not have been produced *earlier* than 1868, even if the pattern dates before that time.

A Marking System

One system that many American Manufactures adopted for marking their flatware used a combination of a letter and a number or just a number.

A1: standard plate
XII: sectional plate
4: double plate on <u>teaspoons</u>
6: double plate on <u>dessert spoons</u> and <u>forks</u>
8: double plate on <u>tablespoons</u>
6: triple plate on <u>teaspoons</u>
9: triple plate on <u>desert spoons</u> and <u>forks</u>
12: triple plate on <u>tablespoons</u>

You might see the words "Quadruple Plated" or "Quadruple Plate" on hollowware such as coffee and tea services. Rather than using a number code, some manufacturers used this as a marketing tool to indicate that their items were high quality.

Some other marks you may see on silver plate are:

AO: Standard
A1: Extra
AA: Double
AAA: Triple

William Rogers and Company used the letter "X" for standard, "XX" for double-plate, and "XXX" for triple plate.

You may even see the words "extra," "extra heavy," "ultra," "double," "triple," and "quadruple."

Sheffield Plate versus Electroplate

1. Electroplating created a film of pure silver that is whiter and harsher looking than the Sterling used on Old Sheffield plate.

2. The layer of pure silver on electroplate has maker's marks and may have other marks indicating the quality of the plate and the base metal used under the plate.

3. Old Sheffield plate was put together from parts that already had a silver top layer. They used soft solder, not silver solder, to join these parts. Soft solder is grayer than the Sheffield plate body. Look carefully at the seams to see if they are darker than the body.

4. Electroplate takes the formed body and coats it with silver. The body, *including* the soldered joints, will have a coat of silver.

5. Electroplate manufacturers were in competition with the high-quality wares of Old Sheffield plate, so electroplate manufacturers used the word "Sheffield" on electroplated items. Expect to find: "Sheffield Silver," "Sheffield Plate," "Sheffield Silver on Copper," or "Sheffield, England" on pieces that are really electroplate and not Old Sheffield plate.

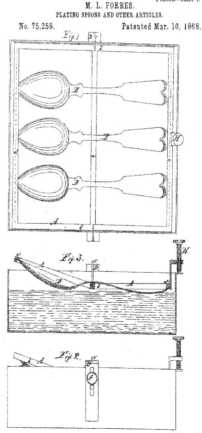

M. L. FORBES.

PLATING SPOONS AND OTHER ARTICLES.

No. 75,258.   Patented Mar. 10, 1868.

2 Sheets—Sheet 1.

Figure 2-7: 1868 Sectional Plating Patent

Silver Substitutes

The Chinese developed a silvery substance that looked like silver around 1595. It was called *paktong*. This silver-looking alloy was a combination of copper, zinc, and nickel. The Chinese managed to keep the process a secret until the late 18th century, when the process was duplicated in Germany. In 1825, Mr. Guitike of Berlin, Germany, went to Sheffield, England, where he introduced the English to his new silvery-colored alloy of copper, zinc and nickel.

With copper-based wares, the orange color would show through when the silverplate wore off. With this new white metal, the wear points were not as obvious when the silver top layer wore off. In 1830, Samuel Robert applied for a patent to plate silver using this white metal base, and it has been used as a base for electroplating ever since. It was called "German Silver" because the formula came from Germany. The name "German Silver" was used in the United States until 1907, when the National Metals Stamping act took effect. This act made it illegal to mark any item with the words "silver, Sterling or coin" if it contained no silver.

There are many names for white base metals with no silver content. Some used the word "silver" until prohibited by U.S. law. Here is a partial list:

Alaska silver
Albata: nickel, copper, and zinc
ALP
Alpaca
Alpacca
Alpaka
Argentan: French for "nickel silver"
Argentine: an alloy of tin and antimony, manufactured in
    1833 by W. Hutton Sons of Sheffield, England
Argentina silver
Arguzoid
Brazil silver: term used by the Globe Nevada Silver
    Works of Birmingham, England
Britannia metal: an alloy that resembles pewter but
    is stronger and more silvery in color
British plate
BP
Crown metal: term used by Yates of Birmingham,
    England

German silver
Neusilber: used in Germany and Scandinavia
Nickel silver
Nevada silver
NS
Paktong
Pot metal
Potosi silver: (South America)
Queen's metal: made by Ashberry of Sheffield, England
Tutania: an alloy of brass, antimony, and tin
White metal
White silver

SILVER PLATED WARE.

SUPERIOR QUALITY, TRIPLE PLATE ON GENUINE ALBATA,

Made and guaranteed by the cele.rated Manufacturers

SIMPSON, HALL, MILLER & CO

No. 24.   WATER SET. $38.00.   Consisting of Tray, Pitcher, and Two Goblets.

Figure 2-8: 1878 Clapp, Young and Company catalog page with a water set of silverplated albata

Figure 2-9: Detail of sugar tongs marked "Nevada Silver"

Figure 2-10: Detail of a spoon marked "Brazil Silver"

Testing Silver

We now know that not everything that looks like silver is silver. Since testing silver takes off some of the metal, testing is not recommended if the piece is marked. Many small items were exempt from hallmarking laws in quite a number of countries, so sometimes your piece may not be marked and testing may be the only way you can tell what the silver content is.

If you do want to test your silver, you need silver testing acid and a notching file, available from a jeweler's supply store.

You will need to file a deep notch in the item to be tested. Next add a drop of the silver testing solution to the notched area.

The solution will change colors, depending on the metal content:

Brass	Dark Brown	Fine Silver	Bright Red
Copper	Brown	925 Silver	Dark Red
Nickel	Blue	800 Silver	Brown
Palladium	None	500 Silver	Green
Gold	None	Lead	Yellow
Tin	Yellow		

Chapter 3: Shaping and Forming Silver

One of the things that makes silver such a useful metal is that it is easy to form. By that we mean that the metal is soft enough to change. As we found in the last chapter, by adding a small amount of an alloy like copper, the combined metals become hard enough to keep the new shape once it has been changed.

We can change the overall shape of a silver piece and we can change the way it is decorated. It is an important part of the identification to be able to tell how the piece is formed.

Raising and Sinking

The first way to give the piece shape is called *raising* or *sinking*. A small metal disk is heated and hammered against a soft surface. After a while, the shape is raised from a flat surface, in the case of Figure 3-1, to a small cup.

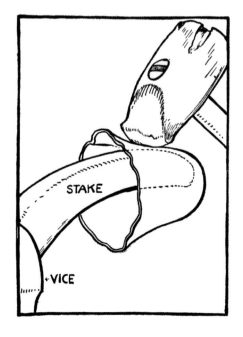

Figure 3-1: Raising a cup, from *The Artistic Crafts Series of Handbooks, No. II. Silverwork and Jewelry*

STAKE

←VICE

Sheet Metal Forming

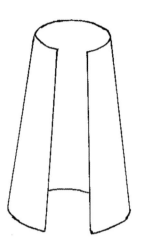

Another way to form a shape is by starting with a sheet of silver. Figure 3-2 shows a diagram of how the sheet is rolled into a tapered cylinder to begin to form the piece.

Figure 3-2: Drawing of a sheet rolled to start the form

Figure 3-3 shows how the sheet is cut to create a joint that will be soldered. The edges are snipped and then laced together. The seam can be soldered and the lines are hammered out.

Figure 3-3: Drawing showing the construction of a butt joint

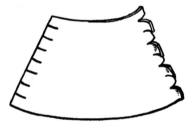

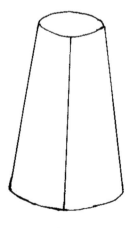

Figure 3-4: Drawing of a piece of sheet with finished edges formed from a butt joint

Figure 3-4 shows the finished cone. Figure 3-5 shows an 18th century coffeepot using the tapered form in the previous illustrations.

Figure 3-5: Tapered coffeepot by William Draker, London hallmarks, 1731 (photo courtesy of www.prices4antiques.com)

Casting Methods

Silver can be melted down and cast – poured into a mold to create the final shape. There are many casting methods. Cast silver pieces will be thicker than sheet metal. That's one of the ways to tell the difference between the two.

When we covered electroplating In Chapter 2, we found that manufacturers silverplated over cast bodies. Cast bodies are thicker than bodies made of sheet. This is why silverplate is usually heavier than Sterling silver pieces.

Sand Casting

The earliest form of casting was *sand casting*. This process involves making a form out of a material such as wood. A box is made to hold the casting sand (called the embedment), which is mixed with a solution that will allow it to harden and hold its shape. The form is pressed into the sand to form the top half of the piece and the process is repeated to make the bottom half of the piece. Figure 3-6 shows a patent for sand casting issued in 1889. Figure 3-7 shows an aluminum factory during World War II with a workman standing by a sand-casting mold.

World War II had a tremendous impact on technology. Manufacturers discovered that it was not necessary to use as fine a casting sand to produce parts.

It is interesting to compare the similarities between the photo in Figure 3-7 and the diagram of a patent issued in 1889 in Figure 3-6. As you can see, the process has not changed much. *It is the quality*

31

of the casting sand that gives us the dating clue. Cast items that were produced after World War II will look much rougher under 10x magnification.

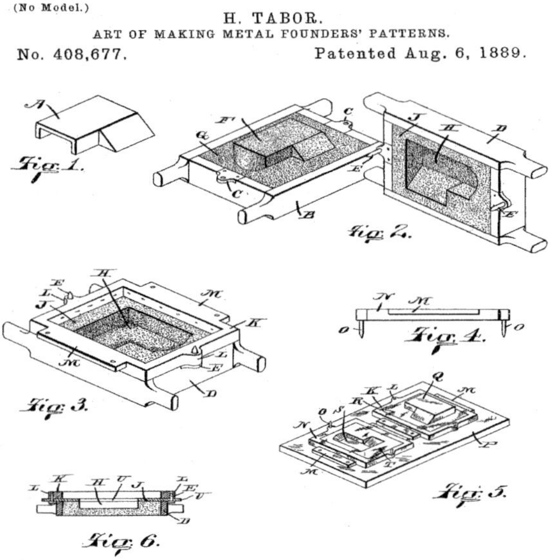

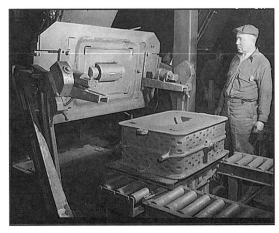

(No Model.)

H. TABOR.

ART OF MAKING METAL FOUNDERS' PATTERNS.

No. 408,677.   Patented Aug. 6, 1889.

Figure 3-6: Patent diagram of a sand casting mold

Figure 3-7: Photograph of a workman by a sand casting mold for airplane parts during World War II

The two pictures in Figure 3-8 show antique cast iron and reproduction cast iron, both at 10x magnification. A comparison of both shows how much more fine the sand was that was used to cast the antique iron.

In practice, when silver is cast, it is hand finished or *planished* to smooth any surface imperfections. Compare Figure 3-8 to Figure 3-9, a piece of cast silver at 10x magnification.

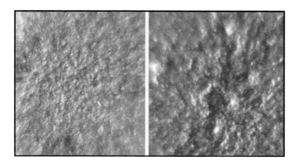

Figure 3-8: Antique casting (left) and new casting (right), both at 10x power

Figure 3-9: Antique cast silver at 10x power

Lost Wax Casting

There is another method of casting using wax to form the mold. Many 19th century silver and silverplate manufacturers used this technique. It is most often used for parts of silver hollowware like feet and decorative accents or other parts that are small, complex or require fine detail. It is also called "investment casting," or the *cire perdue* method. Although this technique was originally used by the Romans over 2,000 years ago, the process was lost and then rediscovered in the late 17th century, about 1675. The main difference is that a wax form is made from a reusable master. The wax form is then fitted into the casting sand. The molten metal is poured into the embedment and the wax melts out. A new wax form is made from the master for additional castings.

Slush Casting

While this method is most often associated with pewter, 18th and 19th century silver manufacturers, as well as Old Sheffield plate manufacturers, used slush casting for such things as coffee pot spouts or feet on teapots. When electroplating was developed in the 19th century, these manufacturers also continued the practice of slush casting smaller parts of their wares. With slush casting, the molten metal is poured into a metal mold. The molten metal immediately begins to cool and harden. While the center is still in liquid form, the metal is poured out. For things like handles and spouts, the inside is never seen, so this process saves money by using less metal.

Elementary Tips on Casting

There are a few things to look for when you look at a piece of cast silver or cast silverplate. Since casting is usually done in sectional molds, the metal while in a molten state can create "fins" in a poorly made mold. Figure 3-10 shows an early patent for an improvement in casting spoons. It shows good pictures of what metal spoon molds looked like. Figure 3-11 shows the foot of a tray cast in a two-piece mold. You can see the fins on the edges of the casting. Inspecting the feet, spout, handles, and edges of flatware gives you the best clues. An antique piece of silver or silverplate should not have large fins.

Sometimes the mold lines (fins) in an antique piece may be slightly visible if there is an area where it is hard to finish (planish) because of the detail of the pattern.

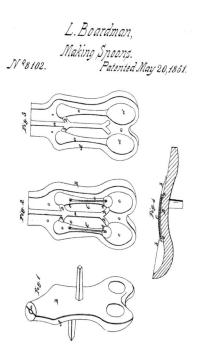

L. Boardman,
Making Spoons.
N°8102. *Patented May 20, 1851.*

Figure 3-12 shows another telltale sign of modern manufacturing, grinding marks. In this picture, the edge of a piece of silver flatware shows where the manufacturer tried to grind off the fins, like those in Figure 3-11. This type of machinery was not used until the early 20th century. Antique silver manufacturers took an additional step in the finishing process, called

Figure 3-10: Patent for casting spoons in a sectional mold, 1851

planishing. Any irregular marks are buffed down unless it looks as if it would be very difficult to finish off or planish. There should not be any sharp edges unless they are part of the pattern.

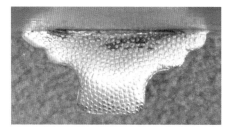

Figure 3-11: Foot of a tray cast in a two-piece mold, fins not removed

Figure 3-12: Grinding marks on the edge of a spoon handle

Antique molds were carefully made. Make sure that the pattern from each side of the mold meets carefully. Figures 3-13, 3-14, and 3-15 show the front, side and back of an antique fork. Notice how the side of the handle is a continuation of the pattern. It does not start on the front, end on the side and start on the back again.

Figure 3-13: Antique fork handle front

Figure 3-14: Antique fork handle back

Figure 3-15: Antique fork handle side

Antique castings for housewares were made more carefully than they are today. The pieces were cast more accurately and finished better. Always look to see if there are mold lines, grinding marks, and fins. You should look on feet, spouts, handles, and applied decorations.

When compared to the antique flatware, the design of the contemporary flatware handle in Figures 3-16 and 3-17 is one-sided. The pattern on the back and the pattern on the front do not meet. It is much less expensive to create a mold like this.

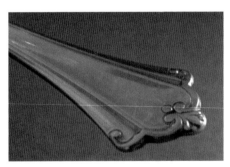

Figure 3-16: Contemporary flatware, one-dimensional design

Figure 3-17: Contemporary flatware, back

Remember that many antique silver flatware patterns are quite plain and do not have a lot of ornamentation. One that comes to mind is called a "fiddleback" pattern, shown in Figure 3-18. In this case, you will need to look for other clues, like grinding marks, fins, and the overall fineness of the casting.

36

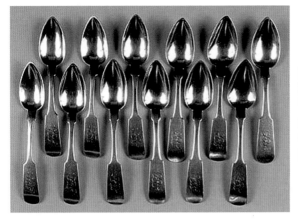

Figure 3-18: Sterling spoons, "Fiddleback" pattern, (courtesy of prices4antiques.com)

Die Stamping

Flatware can be formed by die stamping where rectangular pieces of base metal or silver are given shape when placed between two steel dies. One die contains the top portion of the design and the other, the bottom portion. The base metal is formed into a utensil when pressed between both dies. The finished product is polished to remove any rough edges. Just as with casting, you can inspect the edges to see how well the piece is finished. Grinding marks like those shown in Figure 3-12 are typical of contemporary manufacture. Sometimes, die stamping marks look like grinding marks. They both leave the same type of vertical lines. Manufacturers hand-planished the edges to remove die marks. In either case, you should not expect to see these marks on antique pieces. Evidence of die stamping may be visible in areas that are difficult to finish.

In the early 19th century, this process was called *swaging*. Figure 3-19 shows an 1830 patent for swaging spoons.

Spinning

This technique is associated with tin, copper, and Britannia metal (a type of pewter). With the introduction of silverplate, manufacturers found new ways to cut down on production time. Both tin and pewter are soft metals. With a machine like the one shown in Figure 3-20, metal could be spun and formed into a vessel without seams. A thick circular sheet was placed on a form and turned against that form. As it is turns, the sheet conforms to the shape, "raising" it and

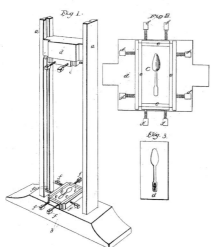

creating an object, such as a bowl, with no seams. If you look at the interior of the piece, it will show circular scoring lines. Sometimes, a small indent is visible on the bottom, directly in the center. This is the axis point where the piece was rotated as it was formed. A change in the alloys used in pewter allowed it to be worked by spinning instead of casting. Since silver is **not** formed this way, this is another clue to help you decide whether your piece is silver.

Figure 3-19: Patent diagram of a machine for swaging spoons, 1830

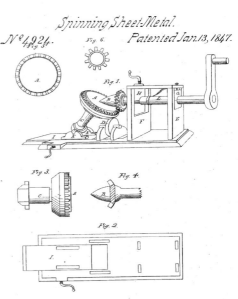

Figure 3-20: Patent diagram for spinning metal, 1847

Putting It Together

Since most hollowware and some flatware are made from several different pieces, the silversmith assembles the various parts to make the final product. The way the piece is put together will also give you clues that help you date it.

Antique silver and silverplate was carefully assembled with no signs of excessive solder. Look around the handles, spouts and feet for signs of solder. Figure 3-21 shows the underside of a circa 1800 coffee-pot foot. You cannot see any excess solder between the foot and the base. Compare this to Figure 3-22, which shows an obvious sloppy bead of solder on the underside of a tray where one foot is attached.

Figure 3-21: Sheffield plate soldered foot

Figure 3-22: Cast foot back with poor soldering

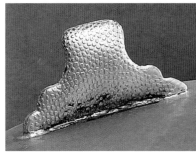

Figure 3-23: Cast foot front

Figure 3-23 shows the front of a foot, with the back of the same foot seen in Figure 3-22. When you compare the front of the foot to the back, you can see that the front has nice little scrolls and the back looks like it has the measles. The manufacturer simply made a rough design (Figure 3-22) that gives the piece a finished look. It takes a lot less time to make a mold if you don't have to worry about whether the front and back match. Most people don't look at the underside of a piece of hollowware. Antique silver will have a smooth look to areas that have no pattern, or the design will be continuous.

When looking at soldered joints, the piece should be joined with *silver* solder. Old Sheffield plate was joined with a soft solder that looks dull gray, not silver. Electroplated wares have a layer of silver *over* the solder. It will be difficult to tell where the solder actually begins. These two points should tell you that your piece may not be silver at all.

Sometimes complex pieces with multiple parts, like candelabrum, will be joined with nuts and bolts rather than solder. This is true with antique and contemporary pieces. A quick inspection of the underside will tell you if the piece was made after the 19th century or not. The square nut was used until about 1900. After that, the hex nut (a six-sided nut) was used.

Figure 3-24: Candelabra bottom

Remember, you will find your best clues on spouts, feet, handles, finials, and lids.

Chapter 4: Hollowware

In this chapter, we will look at how construction techniques changed for silver tableware and how we can use these clues to help identify and date our silver items.

Identifying Hollowware

When we try to identify the style of a piece of silver or silverplate, we are talking about more than just the decorative elements that are applied to the body of the piece. We are talking about the shape, size, and construction differences that have taken place over the centuries. As you will see, the styles have been repeated.

Dating Coffee Pots

Coffee was introduced to England from the Middle East and Turkey. Records show that coffee was consumed as a beverage in England as early as 1637, but the earliest surviving *silver* coffee pot dates to 1681.

Below is a list of assembly techniques that will help you decide how old your coffee pot is. The dates used apply to England and the European continent. Typically, styles came to the United States ten to twenty years later, so you may need to make some time adjustments, depending on where your piece was made.

If you have a piece you are trying to identify, just start at the top with the finial (the handle on top of the lid) and compare your treasure to our clues.

Coffee Pot Finials

Before about 1800 – *Finials* are cast separately and then *soldered* to the top of the coffee pot.

After 1800 – *Cast finials* can also be attached to the lids with threaded shafts and secured with small nuts visible on the interior of the lid.

After 1800 – *Wooden finials* are more common on coffee pots.

Coffee Pot Lids

1680 to about 1730 – Coffee pots have *high-domed lids*. The lid is as wide as the upper body of the coffee pot.

By 1740 – The lid of the coffee pot has changed to a stepped bun shape that is flattened by 1740. (See Figure 4-1.)

Coffee Pot Hinges

1680 to 1800 – The *stand-away hinge* in Figure 4-1 stands well away from the lid. This was done to make cleaning easier. Sometimes, the hinge will come apart so the lid can be removed for easier cleaning.

1800 forward – The *fold-over hinge* was used on coffee pots. Figures 4-2 and 4-3 show coffee pots with fold-over hinges.

Coffee Pot Handles

1680 to about 1805 – Coffee pot handles have *wood or ivory handles* and *pins* that secure the handles to the sockets.

Wooden handles are prone to wear. If they are original to the piece, they should have dark areas where the handle was held. Ivory handles should have dark areas, too. Figure 4-3 is shows an example of a coffee pot with a wooden handle.

About 1805 – *Silver handles* begin to replace wood and ivory handles. They will have wood or ivory insulators like the coffee pot in Figure 4-4.

Coffee Pot Handle Sockets

1680 to 1730 – *Handle sockets* were made of sheet metal and soldered to the body, sometimes with a round reinforcing plate. The sheet seam should be visible.

1730 forward – *Handle sockets* were cast in scroll shapes and soldered to the body of the coffee pot.

Coffee Pot Spouts

Before 1770 – *Spouts* of quality coffee pots will be **cast** in two sections.

From c1770 forward – Mass produced pots are more common. The *spouts* are formed from two pieces of *stamped sheet* and brazed together.

1700s forward – *Spouts* begin to have applied leaf designs. It is sometimes called a *leaf-wrapped spout.* If your coffee pot is a lighthouse shape with a high dome and a *leaf-wrapped* spout, it is probably a reproduction.

Coffee Pot Body Shapes

1680 to about 1740 – Early lighthouse coffee pots have **tapered cylinder-shaped bodies**, made of sheet and seamed together. The seam should be visible beneath the spout area.

1740 to 1825 – The cylinder-shaped body tucks in at the bottom.

c1760 to 1880s – *Pear-shaped* and *inverted pear-shaped* bodies are fashionable. The pear-shape becomes more bulbous and curving in the 1800s.

1770 to 1820 – *Urn-shaped* coffee pots are popular.

1800 to 1820 – Short and squat coffee pots with lobes or gadrooning. Gadrooning is a form of decoration that creates a border that looks like a row of beads on the lower body are popular.

1820s forward – Variations of the pear, urn, and bulbous shape remain popular for coffee pots.

1875 forward – *Lighthouse-shaped* bodies are popular again.

1875 to 1890 – Coffee pots with elongated pear shapes are popular.

Coffee Pot Feet and Bases

1680 to 1770 – The **foot rims** on early coffee pots were *cast* and then soldered to the body.

1770 to 1820 – The **pedestal base** becomes popular.

1800 to 1820 – The *footed* pedestal base makes its appearance.

1820 forward – Expect to see coffee pots with either pedestal bases or feet.

Figure 4-1: 1731 Lighthouse coffee pot by William Draker, James D. Julia Auctions (photo courtesy of prices4antiques.com)

Figure 4-2: 1889 Mermod and Jacquard catalog page showing coffee and tea service

Figure 4-3: 1775-1800 American coffee pot, Rococo style, with large pins holding wooden handles in place, Northeast Auctions (photo courtesy of prices4antiques.com)

Figure 4-4: 1798 English coffee pot, foliate decorations, showing silver handles with heat insulators, Eldred's Auction (photo courtesy of prices4antiques.com)

Figure 4-5: 1752 English coffee pot, lighthouse shape with tucked in bottom, Pook and Pook, Inc. (photo courtesy of prices4antiques.com)

Figure 4-6: 1761 English, Georgian coffee pot, Rococo style, pedestal base, Skinner, Inc. (photo courtesy of prices4antiques.com)

Figure 4-7: 1775 English, Georgian coffee pot, pedestal base, Pook and Pook, Inc. (photo courtesy of prices4antiques.com)

Dating Teapots

The earliest known silver teapot is in the Victoria and Albert Museum in London, England. Fortunately (because it looks a lot like a coffee pot), it was engraved with an inscription and dated 1670.

Teapot Finials

1700 forward – Teapot finials usually mirror the shape of the body.

1700 to about 1800 – Finials are cast separately and then *soldered* to the top of the teapot.

1730 forward – Teapots were made with **wooden finials** much earlier than were coffee pot finials.

1800 forward – **Cast finials** can also be attached to the lids with threaded shafts and secured with small nuts visible on the interior of the lid.

Teapot Lids

1670 to 1730 – Early teapots have **high, dome-shaped lids.** The lid is raised from sheet with no seams or mold lines.

1730 to 1770 – To complement new body shapes, lids are slightly rounded.

1770 forward – The shape of the lid complements the body style. It could be a flattened dome or a tapered lid.

Teapot Hinges

1670 to 1730 – The **stand-away hinge** was used on early pear-shaped teapots.

1725 forward – Flush-set hinges were used. The **"bullet-shaped" teapot** was developed about 1725.

Teapot Handles

1700 to 1740 – Teapots have **wooden handles** and heavy silver pins that secure the handles to the sockets. **Wooden handles** are prone to wear. If they are original to the piece, they should have dark areas where the handle was held. Ivory handles should have dark areas, too.

1730 to 1770 – Some teapots had *cast* silver handles. **Ivory or bone collars** were inserted to prevent the hot water from making the handle too hot to hold.

1810 forward – **Silver handles** were also made of *sheet metal* with ivory or bone insulators.

Teapot Handle Sockets

1680 to 1730 – **Handle sockets** were made of *sheet metal* until about 1730.

1730 to 1770 – **Handle sockets** were *cast* in scroll shapes.

1770 forward – **Handle sockets** are made from sheet metal with both halves seamed together.

Teapot Spouts

1680 to 1770 – **Spouts** of early teapots will be *cast* in two sections. In addition, spouts usually have tiny lids to help keep the heat in.

1770 forward – **Spouts** are made from *sheet metal* and seamed.

Teapot Strainers

1680 to 1770 – **Pierced strainers** were *soldered* to the opening of the spout on the inside of the pot until about **1730**.

1770 forward – The body of the teapot is pierced. The opening of the spout is soldered over the pierced area of the body.

Teapot Shapes

1680 to 1730 – Because tea was very expensive, early teapots were very small, about 4½ to 6" high, holding only one or two cups.

1680 to 1730 – Body shapes were either lighthouse forms with tucked-in bottoms or pear-shaped.

1710 to 1725 – A fashionable change in body construction is popular, in which the body shapes are formed with octagonal panels. This involves a lot of labor, so this form is seldom reproduced. The example in Figure 4-8 is a kettle on a stand and dates to 1788, but the idea is still the same. Reproductions are more likely to be made in forms that are easier to reproduce.

1730 to 1770 – The bullet-shaped teapot body is popular.

1740 to 1800 – The inverted pear-shaped body is popular.

1780 to 1795 – The drum-shaped body is popular.

1800 to 1820 – Short and squat teapots with lobes or gadrooning on the lower body are popular.

1810 forward – Improvement in rolling mills allows manufacturers to roll silver sheet much thinner. Teapot **bodies** become much thinner.

1820s forward – Variations of the pear, urn, and bulbous shape remain popular for teapots. Complete coffee and tea services are very common with coffee pots and teapots made in the complimentary shapes.

Teapot Foot Rims

1700 to 1770 – **Foot rims** were made separately, usually cast and soldered to the body of the teapot.

Figure 4-8: 1788 English kettle-on-stand by Hester Bateman, Sterling, Skinner, Inc. (photo courtesy of www.prices4antiques.com)

Figure 4-9: English bullet-shaped teapot, Sterling, early 18th century, Brunk Auctions (photo courtesy of www.prices4antiques.com)

Dating Creamer Pitchers and Milk Jugs

In the late 17th century, tea was generally served with sugar, not milk or cream. Before the development of pasteurization, drinking fresh, cold milk was unsafe, causing disease and sometimes death. Cream pitchers dating back to this time period were used for dessert services. Serving fresh cream over fruit was a common delicacy on farms and rural areas, where the freshness of the cream could be easily determined.

1710 forward – Matching milk jugs are made for tea services.

1780 forward – Matching cream pitchers are made for tea services.

You are probably thinking, "What's the difference?" That's a very good question.

Hot milk jugs from this time may have a lid to keep in the heat. The spout is pointed to allow control of the amount of milk poured. Early jugs are footed to prevent the hot body from touching the table surface. Later, the pedestal base was used.

Tea was served with cold milk by 1727. Rather than a beak-shape, the lip was curved and a little wider. Rococo styles popular at this time went better with a curved lip, rather than a beak-shaped lip.

Cream pitchers have very wide lips to allow slow pouring of the cream.

Figure 4-10: 1751-1761 American, coin silver hot milk jug, Brunk Auctions (photo courtesy of prices4antiques.com)

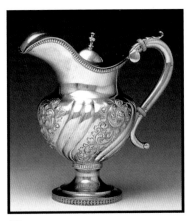

Coffee was a much stronger beverage. It was believed that milk or cream softened the effects of tannin and caffeine. Because of this, coffee was usually served with hot milk or cream. You can find early coffee pots with matching cream pitchers and milk jugs.

Figure 4-11: 1820–1858 American, coin silver, hot milk jug with lid, Neal Auction Company (photo courtesy of prices4antiques.com)

50

Figure 4-12: 1763 –1770 England, George III, cream pitcher, Brunk Auctions (photo courtesy of prices4antiques.com)

1700s – Both hot milk jugs and cream pitchers were raised from sheet with no seams.

1810 forward – As with teapots, improvements in rolling mills allowed thinner sheet to be used to make jugs and pitchers.

If the pitcher has wood or ivory handles, it is intended for serving hot beverages.

Dating Tea and Coffee Services

Early 1700s – Tea services contained only a teapot and sugar bowl.

1790 forward – Taking tea with sugar and *cream* becomes more common. By this time, a tea service consisted of the teapot, sugar bowl, and creamer (or milk jug). Shortly after that, coffee pots were added to the sets.

1800s forward – Complete six-piece tea services were made. They included a kettle and a waste bowl. This is a useful dating clue if you are fortunate to find an old set with all of its components.

1850 forward – By the time of the Great Exhibition in 1851, manufacturers were advertising silver teas services with *matching trays*. (See Figure 4-13.)

Dating Wine Coasters, Decanter Stands, and Wine Wagons

In the early 18th century, wine or port was served from bottles after dinner in the drawing room. Servants would uncork the bottles and serve the beverage in goblets.

Figure 4-13: Engraving of a tea and coffee set from the Great Exhibition of 1851

It was difficult to have intimate conversations in the presence of servants. There are historical accounts of servants who used information overheard during these gatherings to blackmail their employers.

Eventually, the custom of personal service of wine developed, excluding the presence of servants. The bottle was slid around the table from host to guest.

Wine coasters were developed to prevent the bottles (sometimes chipped) from scratching wooden tabletops. They were originally called *bottle sliders* and *bottle stands*.

Wine Coasters

Mid 1700s forward – Wine coasters have been developed for private wine service. At this time they were solid silver and raised from one piece. The bottoms were slightly convex, making it easier to slide the coaster across the table. They tended to be straight-sided and about four inches in diameter.

Figure 4-14: 1794 George III wine coasters, Sterling, 5" diameter, Brunk Auctions (photo courtesy of prices4antiques.com)

By 1760 – Wine coasters are made of two-piece construction. Shortly after that, a lathe-turned wooden base developed. It prevented the bottom of the bottle from sticking to the coaster.

1800 forward – Changes in bottle design affected the size of wine coasters. The diameter decreased to about 3½", and the height increased to complement the new narrow, taller bottle.

Decanter Stands

1787 – **Decanter stands** came into use. Decanter stands were wider than bottle stands, about 5" in diameter, as decanters tended to have a wider base. The rims of decanter stands flare out.

1790s forward – **Double** decanter stands came into use. They held two bottles in one stand.

By 1800 – The height of decanter stands is about half the height of wine coasters.

Figure 4-15: Unattributed Sheffield decanter stand, 5¼" diameter, late 1700s, Brunk Auctions (photo courtesy of prices4antiques.com)

Figure 4-16: 1825 English Sheffield plate wine wagon, Skinner, Inc. (photo courtesy of prices4antiques.com)

Wine Wagons

About 1882 – Wine wagons are made. These wagons had wheels and a handle so that the wine could be rolled around the table in its stand.

Wine coasters, decanter stands, and wine wagons were usually sold in quantities of two, four, or more. The value of a pair of coasters or stands is substantially more than if they were sold independent of one another.

Popular Hollowware Patterns

Six hollowware patterns, all of which have matching flatware, have been popular since they were introduced. They are shown below.

As you can see from Figures 4-22 and 4-23, there are two different Wallace *Rose Point* patterns. Both are available in silver and silverplate. There are also different *Repoussé* patterns with varying amounts of raised decorations.

Figure 4-17: *Chantilly* pattern by Gorham, introduced in 1895 (photo courtesy of replacements.com)

Figure 4-18: *Fairfax* pattern by Durgin, introduced in 1910 (photo courtesy of replacements.com)

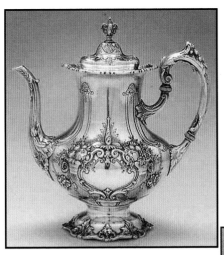

Figure 4-19: *Francis I* pattern by Reed and Barton, introduced in 1907 (photo courtesy of replacements.com)

Figure 4-20 (above) and 4-21 (left): *Repoussé* pattern, by Kirk Stieff, introduced in 1828 (photo courtesy of replacements.com)

Figure 4-22: *Rose Point* pattern by Wallace, introduced in 1934 (photo courtesy of replacements.com)

Figure 4-23: *Rose Point* pattern by Wallace, introduced in 1934 (photo courtesy of replacements.com)

Figure 4-24: *Strasbourg* pattern by Gorham, introduced in 1897 (photo courtesy of replacements.com)

Chapter 5: Flatware

Dating Flatware

Here in the United States, our construction techniques and styles usually begin later than in England and the European continent. We were across the ocean. Our styles were often up to 20 years behind other countries. We talk more about this in the chapter on styles, but for now just try to give yourself a date range instead of trying to pin things to an exact time.

Forks

Forks were originally developed to serve meat. They were two-pronged, made of iron, and used from the 14th century. The Italians are given credit for using forks for dining. The custom caught on rather slowly in England, where eating with a fork was considered unmanly.

1400s – **Two- and four-pronged forks** were developed.

1600s – **Three-pronged forks** were developed.

Late 1700s – **Dessert forks** (smaller than a place knife) became popular. They often had a handle of bone, amber, or tortoise shell. The preference for these types of handles continues until about **1900**.

Before 1800 – *Silver* forks were made of two-piece construction.

After 1800 – Forks made of *iron* and other base metals continue to be made in two-piece construction well into the 19th century.

Late 1840s – *Silver* place forks do not appear to be commonplace on the dinner table. Etiquette books from this period recommend silver forks *if possible* instead of steel forks for formal dinners.

Spoons

While the first eating utensil was the knife (spear it and eat it), the spoon was the next utensil to make its way to the dinner table. They are in common use by about 1650.

1660 to 1760 – "Rat-tail" spoons are common. Look for a "rat-tail" at the back of the bowl. It was intended to add strength to the joint between the bowl and the stem.

Figure 5-1: 17th century "rat-tail" spoon

Before 1700 – Spoons were hand hammered into a lead die. The handle or stem was attached afterwards and will have an irregular appearance.

Before 1800 – Spoons were made of two-piece construction, as was most flatware. The handle is attached to the bowl ending in a small "v". The bowl is very large by today's standards.

Figure 5-2: Spoon back showing two piece construction, about 1800

Before 1830 - Designs were *stamped* on the back of the bowl, usually resembling a lace pattern.

After 1830 - Most *silver* spoons after this date were **cast**. The design was made as part of the mold.

Flatware Stems

Over the centuries, the stem shape on a piece of flatware has changed.

1720 to about 1780 - The stem is straight and the tip tilts up at the end (Figure 5-3, 5-4, and 5-5).

1780 to 1865 -The handle of the flatware will curve down towards the table (Figure 5-6 and 5-7).

1865 forward - The serpentine-shaped handle is in common use by this time. The handle curves upward from the bowl, back towards the table surface and turns back up again. This shape has been used continuously to the present day (Figure 5-8).

58

Handles are an important dating clue. Even if you do not remember all of the dates, you can lay-out dozens of pieces of silver flatware and pick out the pieces that do not lay on the table the way the majority do. You can be sure that those "odd" pieces pre-date the American Civil War.

Figure 5-3:
18th century fork

Figure 5-4: 1820s
Norwegian silver
spoon

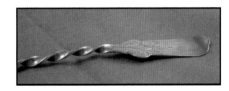

Figure 5-5: Detail, Norwegian silver spoon

Figure 5-6: Hester Bateman
stuffing spoon, 1783

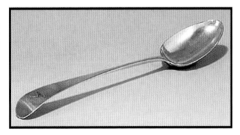

Figure 5-7: John
Round and Sons,
c1860

Figure 5-8: Sterling sugar spoon with a serpentine handle, late 19th century

Serving Pieces

Some serving pieces have earlier dates of use, while others appear early in the 20th century. They are listed below along with probable dates of introduction ("c" means "circa," or "about"):

> Asparagus Tongs: c1790
> Bacon Forks: c1910
> Baked Potato Forks: c1910
> Claret Spoons: 1880s to c1910
> Corkscrews (worms): mid 17th century
> Fish Forks: c1850
> Fish Knives: 1821
> Fish Set (trowel and serving fork): c1820
> Fish Trowel: c1760
> Marrow Spoons: late 1600s through early 1900s.
> Salt Spoons (oval bowl): 1750
> Salt Spoons (trowel shaped bowl): until c1750
> Sugar Tongs: 1690s
> Tea Scoop or Caddy Spoons: 1730s
> Tea Tongs: 1760s.
> Toasting Forks: late 1600s

While manufacturers used different patterns, the function of the pieces they made cause the designs to appear similar. For example, lemon forks are short (usually between 4" and 6" long). They generally have two or three tines with the outer tines curving outward to make it easier to secure a wedge. Strawberry forks have long tines (usually three). Since strawberries can be very large, long tines are necessary to hold the strawberry while it is sliced.

Patented Serving Pieces

While a patent number does not guarantee the first use of a process, it gives us a good idea of the approximate date that a piece began to be used.

The following is a list of the earliest patents we have found for important developments in the flatware and hollowware industry along with their patent office diagrams.

Figure 5-9: Corn Skewers patented in 1877 (patent number 187,363)

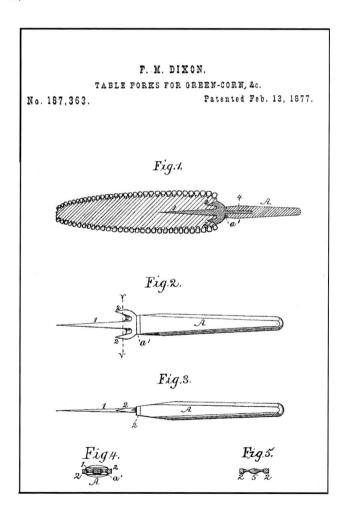

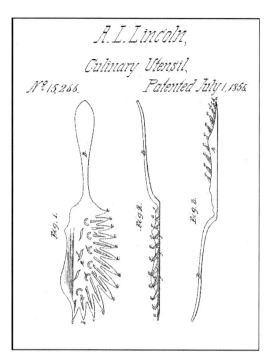

Figure 5-10: Patent office diagram of a macaroni server, 1856 (patent number 15,266)

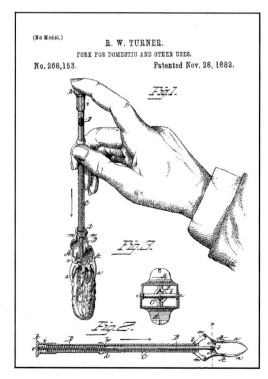

Figure 5-11: Patent office diagram of a mechanical pickle fork, 1882 (patent number 268,153)

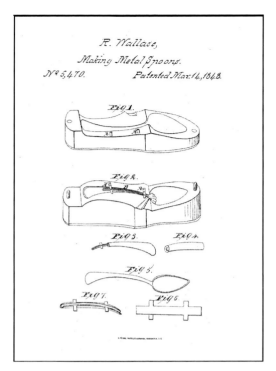

**Figure 5-12:
Reinforced wire along
the spoon handle,
patented in 1848
(Patent number 5,470)**

**Figure 5-13: Tea Ball
and Spoon, patented
in 1891 (Patent num-
ber 453,972).**

This handy device
combines the useful-
ness of a spoon with a
tea ball (patent number
453,972).

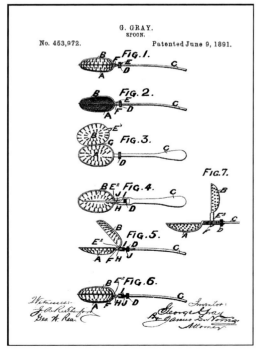

Silver Inlay: First patented in 1884, these patents cover a process to inlay *solid silver* at heavy wear points of silverplated flatware. Look for the words "silver inlay" (patent number 309,013 and patent number 307,099 filed in 1886).

Figure 5-14: Flatware Detail: Edwards Sterling Inlaid

You might even find pieces with patent numbers on them. Keep in mind that a patent number on a piece means the *earliest* date for the piece. It does not automatically mean that your piece is that old, but it's a good starting place.

Dating Tableware and Serving Pieces

Etiquette books from the early 19th century reference little more than dinner forks, dessert spoons, fish knives, dinner knives, dessert spoons, and soup spoons. It appears that there was some confusion about how and when to use these pieces, so special reference was made to them. For instance, one book insisted that peas should be eaten with the dessert spoon.

Most of the pieces we think of as modern serving pieces were in common use by 1890, the majority having been introduced sometime after the American Civil War. While we cannot give exact dates, entries from 19th century catalogs show how serving pieces were added as the century progressed.

1851 The Great Exhibition: London, England

Figure 5-15 is a catalog page from the Great Exhibition of 1851. It shows engravings from some of the contributors. Pictured, starting from upper left, are ivory and Sterling knife handles, skewer handle (below), ice tongs and ice spoon (center), sugar tongs (top right), taper stick, and a fish-carving fork (bottom). The catalog mentions that ice is quite a delicacy, implying that ice tongs and spoons would be available only to the very wealthy.

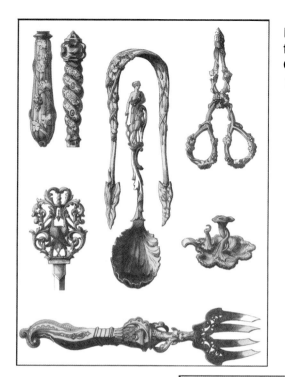

Figure 5-15: Silver flatware from the Great Exhibition of 1851

The catalog page shows silverplated designs for dessert forks, dessert spoons (top left and top right), a cream ladle (center top), a teaspoon and an egg spoon (bottom center, left to right), and tea-caddy spoons (bottom left and right).

Figure 5-16: Silver-plated flatware from the Great Exhibition of 1851

Fish sets, introduced around 1820, are still in style by 1851. Figure 5-17 shows a fish set and dessert knife.

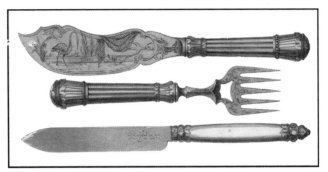

Figure 5-17: Silver fish set and dessert knife from the Great Exhibition of 1851

1875 Montgomery Ward Catalog: Silverplate and Coin Silver

Still a very young company, Montgomery Ward published a mail-order catalog from which rural families could purchase household items. While only a few items were listed, it still gives us an idea of what was available for the rural homemaker in 1875.

Silverplate
Butter Knives
Carving Forks
Carving Knives
Fruit Knives
Gravy Ladles
Soup Ladles
Table Forks
Table Spoons
Tea Spoons

Coin Silver
Napkin Rings
Fruit Knives

1878 Clapp, Young and Company Catalog: Silver and Silverplate

Following are engravings from the Clapp, Young, and Company catalog of 1878. These pages show different types of serving pieces available in silver and silverplate by 1878. As you would expect, less variety is offered in silver, because the prices for silver were still generally out of reach for the average American family.

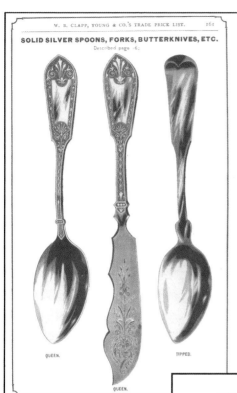

Figure 5-18: Silver spoons and knife in the *Queen* pattern and *Tipped* Pattern, Clapp, Young, and Company, 1878

Figure 5-19: List of silver flatware for sale from Clapp, Young, and Company, 1878

SOLID SILVER GOODS.

PRICE PER DOZ. NET.

Solid Silver Tea Spoons Tipped. Illustrated page 161. Weighing 7 ounces			9	"	$12 25
"	"	"	9	"	15 00
"	Table " same pattern as Tipped Tea. Page 161.	"	14	"	24 50
"	"	"	18	"	30 00
"	" Forks "	"	13	"	23 20
"	"	"	16½	"	28 00
"	Tea Spoons. Queen pattern. Illustrated "	"	8	"	16 00
"	"	"	10	"	18 75
"	Table "	"	16	"	32 00
"	"	"	20	"	37 50
"	" Forks "	"	15	"	31 50
"	"	"	18½	"	35 50
"	Butter Knives—Tipped, $3.00; Queen, $4.00 each.				

SILVER FRUIT KNIVES WITH NUT PICKS.

Illustrated page 164. Prices per dozen, net.

Nos.   49   51   8   7   7 without Pick-
$18 00, 16 50, 14 00, 11 25, 8 50

COIN SILVER NAPKIN RINGS.

Illustrated pages 163 and 164. Price per dozen, net.

Nos. 71   100   4   11   67   57   51   18   87   96
$8 50, 11 00, 12 00, 12 00, 14 00, 16 50, 16 50, 20 00, 22 00, 25 00
14   8   4   78   16   78   69
26 00, 26 00, 28 50, 39 00, 38 00, 50 00, 50 00, 60 00

Coin Silver Child's Set. Illustrated page 159 ....$8 00 each, net.
"   "   Card Case.   "   160 .... 6 00 "   "
"   "   Tobacco Box, Gold lined. Illustrated page 160 ....13 00 "   "

SILVER PLATE CALL BELLS.

Price per dozen, List.

200
13.00 List.

2250
33.00 List.

7300
36.00

8075
19.50 List.

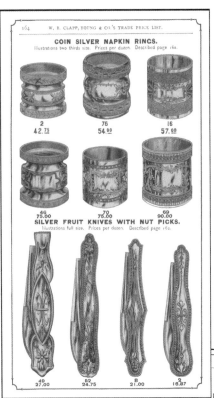

Figure 5-20: Napkin rings, fruit knives, and nut picks, Clapp, Young, and Company, 1878

Figure 5-21: Rogers & Brothers Flatware, Clapp, Young, and Company, 1878

W. B. CLAPP, YOUNG & CO.'S TRADE PRICE LIST. 167

ROGERS & BRO.'S FLAT WARE.

Patterns on page 166, in "Extra" and Triple Plate.

EXTRA PLATE, A 1.

	Plain.	Tipped.	Olive.	Persian	Lily.	Crown.
Tea Spoons, Extra Plate, A 1	$4.00	$4.25	$4.75	$4.75	$4.75	$4.75
Dessert " " " "	7.00	7.50	8.50	8.50	8.50	8.50
Table " " " "	8.00	8.50	9.50	9.50	9.50	9.50
Salt " " " "		3.75	4.25	4.25	4.25	4.25
Mustard " " " "		4.25	4.75	4.75	4.75	4.75
Bar " Long Twist, Extra Plate, A 1		8.50				
Cream Ladles, Extra Plate, A 1		10.50	13.50	13.50	13.50	13.50
Gravy " " " "		15.00	18.00	18.00	18.00	18.00
Soup " " " "		45.00	51.00	51.00	51.00	51.00
Sugar Shells, " " "		6.50	9.00	9.00	9.00	9.00
Pie Knives, " " "			42.00	42.00	42.00	42.00
Butter Knives, Flat Handle, Ex. Plate, A 1			9.00	9.00	9.00	9.00
" " Twist " " "			10.50	10.50	10.50	10.50
Pickle Forks, Extra Plate, A 1		6.50	7.50	7.50	7.50	7.50
Dessert " " " "		7.50	8.50	8.50	8.50	8.50
Medium " " " "		8.50	9.50	9.50	9.50	9.50

TRIPLE PLATE.

	Plain.	Tipped.	Olive.	Persian	Lily.	Crown.
Tea Spoons, Triple Plate, No. 6	$6.50	$6.75	$7.25	$7.25	$7.25	$7.25
Dessert " " " " 9	11.00	11.50	12.50	12.50	12.50	12.50
Table " " " " 12	13.00	13.50	14.50	14.50	14.50	14.50
Salt " " " " 6		6.25	6.75	6.75	6.75	6.75
Mustard " " " " 6		6.75	7.25	7.25	7.25	7.25
Cream Ladles, " " " 12		16.50	19.50	19.50	19.50	19.50
Gravy " " " " 12		24.00	27.00	27.00	27.00	27.00
Soup " " " " 12		69.00	75.00	75.00	75.00	75.00
Sugar Shells, " " " 9		10.50	13.00	13.00	13.00	13.00
Pie Knives, " " " 12			60.00	60.00	60.00	60.00
Butter " Flat Handle, Triple Plate, No. 9			13.00	13.00	13.00	13.00
" " Twist " " " " 9			14.50	14.50	14.50	14.50
Pickle Forks, Triple Plate, No. 9		9.50	10.50	10.50	10.50	10.50
Dessert " " " " 9		11.50	12.50	12.50	12.50	12.50
Medium " " " " 12		13.50	14.50	14.50	14.50	14.50

ROGERS & BRO.'S MEDIUM AND DESSERT KNIVES.

PRICE PER DOZ. NET.

Quadruple Plate, Solid Steel, Medium Knives, No. 16 .... $6 00
" " " " Dessert " " 16 .... 5 50
Triple " " " Medium " " 12 .... 4 75
" " " " Dessert " " 12 .... 4 25
Child's Knife, Fork and Spoon, in Fancy Paper Box .... each, 1 35
" " " " " " Morocco Box 2 00

The above Child's Sets come in Olive, Persian, Lily and Crown.

1889 Mermod and Jaccard Catalog: Silver and Silverplate

Advertising full sets in eight patterns, Mermod and Jaccard guaranteed consumers that their "solid silver" was .925 fineness, showing the continuing trend towards the Sterling standard.

Solid Silver

Almond Spoons	Fish Knives	Pie Forks
Asparagus Forks	Fruit Knives	Pie Knives
Berry Spoons	Grape Shears	Preserve Spoons
Bon-Bon Spoons	Gravy Ladles	Punch Ladles
Butter Knives	Ice Cream Forks	Salad Forks
Butter Picks	Ice Cream Server	Salad Spoons
Cake Knives	Ice Cream Spoons	Salt Spoons (individual)
Carving Fork	Ice Spoons	Sardine Forks
Carving Knives	Ice Tongs	Sauce Ladles
Cheese Scoops	Jelly Spoons	Soup Ladles
Child's Set Coffee Spoons	Lettuce Forks	Sugar Sifters
Cold Meat Forks	Napkin Rings	Sugar Spoons
Cream Ladles	Olive Forks	Sugar Tongs
Crumb Knives	Orange Spoons	Table Forks
Dessert Forks	Oyster Forks	Tea Spoons
Dessert Knives	Oyster Ladles	Waffle Knives
Fish Forks	Pickle Forks	

Silverplate

Asparagus Forks	Coffee Spoons	Fish Knives
Asparagus Tongs	Cream Ladles	Fruit Knives
Berry Spoons	Crumb Knives	Grape Shears
Butter Knives (individual)	Dessert Forks	Gravy Ladles
Carving Sets	Dessert Spoons	Ice Cream Knives
Cheese Scoops	Fish Forks	Ice Spoons

Silverplate

Ice Tongs	Pie Knives	Sugar Spoons
Knife Rests	Preserve Spoons	Sugar Tongs
Nut Picks and Cracks	Salad Forks	Table Forks
Oyster Forks	Salad Spoons	Table Spoons
Oyster Ladles	Soup Ladles	Tea Spoons
Pickle Forks	Sugar Shells	Waffle Knives
Pie Cutters	Sugar Sifters	

We also carry a full line in all these patterns of

Butter Knives,	Salad Forks,
$3.50 to $6.00	$12.00 to $25.00
Pie Knives,	Lettuce Forks,
$10.00 to $20.00	$5.00 to $10.00
Cake Knives,	Cold Meat Forks,
$10.00 to $20.00	$5.00 to $15.00
Fish Knives,	Fish Forks,
$12.00 to $25.00	$12.00 to $25.00
Crumb Knives,	Asparagus Forks,
$20.00 to $30.00	$14.00 to $25.00
Waffle Knives,	Pickle Forks,
$8.00 to $15.00	$3.00 to $5.00
Fruit Knives,	Olive Forks,
$1.25 to $7.00	$3.50 to $5.00
Dessert Knives, per doz.	Sardine Forks,
$40.00 to $60.00	$3.50 to $8.00
Sugar Spoons,	Oyster Forks, per doz.
$2.75 to $5.00	$15.00 to $30.00
Jelly Spoons,	Ice Cream Forks, pr dz.
$4.00 to $7.00	$25.00 to $45.00
Preserve Spoons,	Pie Forks, per doz.
$7.00 to $12.00	$22.00 to $60.00
Berry Spoons,	Soup Ladles,
$10.00 to 25.00	$15.00 to $45.00
Bon-Bon Spoons,	Oyster Ladles,
$2.50 to $5.00	$12.00 to $20.00
Almond Spoons,	Gravy Ladles,
$4.00 to $7.00	$5.00 to $10.00
Ice Spoons,	Sauce Ladles,
$12.00 to $20.00	$5.00 to $12.00
Ice Cream Spoons, doz.	Cream Ladles,
$25.00 to $50.00	$3.00 to $7.50
Coffee Spoons, per doz.	Punch Ladles,
$10.00 to $27.00	$18.00 to $30.00
Orange Spoons, per dz.	Ice Tongs,
$24.00 to $36.00	$16.00 to $30.00
Salad Spoons,	Butter Picks, per doz.
$12.00 to $25.00	$25.00 to $30.00
Cheese Scoops,	Sugar Tongs,
$8.00 to $15.00	$2.00 to $10.00
Grape Shears,	Sugar Sifters,
$15.00 to $22.00	$5.00 to $12.00

Figure 5-22: Mermod and Jaccard 1889 catalog showing a list of items offered for sale

Figure 5-23: Mermod and Jaccard 1889 catalog showing silverplated pie knife, berry spoon, and cake knife

Figure 5-24: Mermod and Jaccard 1889 catalog showing a versatile silverplated piece that can serve as an ice cream knife, pudding knife, or fish fork

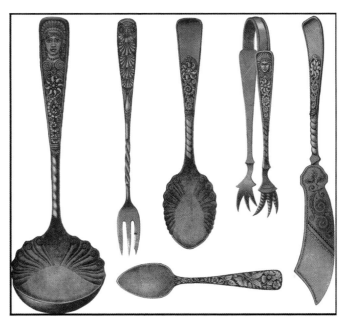

Figure 5-25: Mermod and Jaccard 1889 catalog showing a ladle, oyster fork, sugar shell, sugar tongs, butter knife, and small coffee spoon, all silverplated

1898 Baird-North Company Silver

Late 19th century silver discoveries in America and throughout the world, brought the price of silver down, making silver more affordable. Such manufacturers as Baird-North were now able to offer a wider variety of Sterling silver to the public. Baird-North offered five patterns in this catalog. The following is a list of silver serving pieces offered in their 1898-1899 catalog:

Silver

Beef Forks	Dessert Forks	Pea Spoons
Berry Forks	Dessert Spoons	Pickle Forks
Berry Spoons	Food Pushers	Pie Knives
Butter Knife Picks	Grape Shears	Pie Servers
Butter Picks	Gravy Ladles	Salad Serving Forks
Cheese Picks	Horse Radish Spoons	Sardine Forks
Cheese Scoops	Ice Cream Spoons	Soup Spoons
Children's Forks Tongs	Jelly Knives	Sugar or Bon-Bon
Children's Knives	Jelly Spoons	Sugar Spoons
Children's Spoons	Lettuce Forks	Table Forks
Coffee Spoons	Mustard Spoons	Table Spoons
Cold Meat Forks	Napkin Rings	Tea Spoons
Cork Screws (Sterling handles)	Olive Forks	Tomato Servers
Cream Ladles	Oyster Forks	Vegetable Forks
Cucumber Servers	Pap Spoons	Waffle Knives

As you can see from the illustrations, most of the serving pieces we have today were in use by the end of the 19th century.

Dating Flatware Patterns

Although we have not talked about pricing, a Sterling teaspoon in almost any pattern currently ranges from $15 to $40. You can make your own comparison to the auction prices shown in the next section for a spoon in the *Dog Nose* pattern.

Dog Nose Pattern

1660 to 1760 – Occasionally, a very early pattern called a *Dog Nose* comes up for auction in the United States. The *Dog Nose* spoon (Figure 5-27) auctioned at Sloan's Auction Galleries in Washington, DC for $517 in 2000.

Figure 5-26: *Athena* pattern, Baird-North 1898 catalog showing a wide variety of Sterling flatware serving pieces

Figure 5-27: *Dog Nose* spoon, 1690 to 1700 (photo courtesy of prices4antiques.com)

Tipped (Tipt) Pattern

1712 forward – One of the oldest and most common patterns is called *Tipt* or *Tipped*. It is pictured below. There were many variations made. In England, the same pattern is called *Hanoverian*. The *Tipped* pattern is still made today. Most major American manufacturers have some variation of this pattern. Notice that the engraving in Figure 5-18 and the picture in Figure 5-28 are both the *Tipped* pattern, but made one hundred years apart.

Figure 5-28: Spoon with *Hanoverian* or *Tipped* pattern handle, c1775 (photo courtesy of prices4antiques.com)

1730 forward – **Matching sets of forks and spoons** are common and continue to be made until the late 19th century.

Fiddle-back Pattern

1800s forward – The *Fiddle-back* pattern makes an appearance and continues to be made today. It was made in both England and here in the United States.

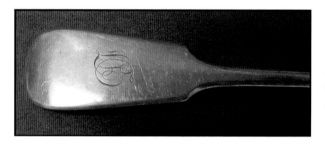

Figure 5-29: c1860 *fiddle-back* spoon

1740 forward – The shell motif, originally used with the Fiddle-back pattern, does not appear to be used before about 1740, but has been used <u>*continuously*</u> since that time.

Figure 5-30: *Fiddle-back* spoon with shell pattern

While we have found a handful of patents for flatware patterns that date before the American Civil War, the majority of US patents are registered between 1890 and 1905. Keep in mind that the US Patent Office was established in 1790. It burned down in 1812 and was rebuilt in 1836. Early patent records were lost in the fire. In addition, not all manufacturers registered their patterns, so there will always be some mystery patterns out there.

Popular Flatware Patterns

In the last chapter, we listed six hollowware patterns that have been popular since they were introduced. Those patterns also have matching flatware, as shown in figures 5-31 through 5-36.

Figure 5-31: *Chantilly* pattern by Gorham, introduced in 1895

Figure 5-32: *Francis I* pattern by Reed and Barton, introduced in 1907

Figure 5-33: *Fairfax* pattern by Durgin, introduced in 1910

Figure 5-34: *Strasbourg* pattern by Gorham, introduced in 1897

Figure 5-35: *Repoussé* pattern, by Kirk Stieff, introduced in 1828

Figure 5-36: *Rose Point* pattern by Wallace, introduced in 1934

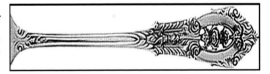

Aside from matching hollowware, another reason these patterns have been popular is that with the exception of *Francis I*, all these patterns are made in silverplate, too.

Silver flatware prices are also affected by supply and demand. The more pieces there are, the less each costs. Look at a typical flatware service for ten. There will be ten place knives, ten place forks, ten salad or fish forks, ten soup spoons, and usually twenty teaspoons. Teaspoons are used for coffee, tea, and some desserts. Most people order extra teaspoons. Manufacturers make more teaspoons, and the teaspoon is usually one of the least expensive pieces in the service.

Individual butter knives also double as serving knives. Most services will have extra individual butter knives, and they are usually the least expensive piece in the flatware service.

Many 19th century retailers made "bridal sets" that had just teaspoons, or serving pieces. Figure 5-37 shows the 1889 Mermod and Jaccard catalog page advertising different pieces boxed as bridal sets.

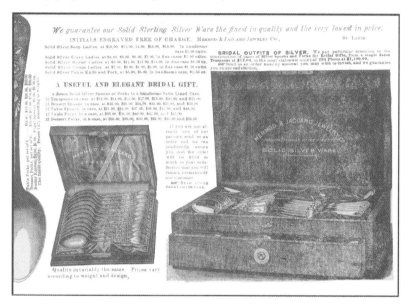

Figure 5-37: Mermod and Jaccard catalog detail of a bridal set, 1889

Most flatware services will have one or two cold meat forks, two or three vegetable serving forks, and two sizes of cream or gravy ladles. Because manufacturers make fewer of these, they cost more than place settings. The more unusual the serving piece, the more it can cost. It is not a function of the price of the silver, its age, or complexity that sets the price.

Since serving pieces cost so much more, many people bought silverplated serving pieces to go with their silver flatware services. This is still a common practice.

If you plan to buy an antique or "vintage" silver service, always remember to *check all the serving pieces to make sure they are silver and not silverplate.*

You can use a silver flatware pattern book to identify many silverplatepatterns and vice versa.

If you are investing in your first silver flatware service, you can take advantage of this, too. You can buy silverplated serving pieces until you can add the solid silver pieces you want.

Some Help with 19th Century Patterns

Many manufacturers sold unmarked flatware to retailers and other manufacturers who then marked the pieces with their own names. Some manufacturers had limited abilities to produce a variety of patterns and pieces. Buying from other manufacturers solved this problem for them.

Retailers looking for a competitive advantage would make up their own pattern names and put their own trade names on both flatware and hollowware. Because of this, it's common to find identical pieces with different manufacturers' names and different company names. Figure 5-38 is from a Mermod and Jaccard catalog dating to 1889. Following this figure is a list of the real pattern names and manufacturers for many of the patterns they advertised at the time.

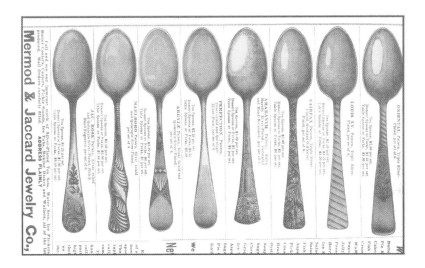

Figure 5-38: Mermod and Jaccard 1889 catalog with trade names for flatware patterns

Oriental: *Assyrian* by 1847 Rogers, introduced in 1887
Louis XV: *Dundee* by 1847 Rogers, introduced in 1886
Fairfax: *Embossed* by 1847 Rogers, introduced in 1882
Argyle: *Peerless* by 1847 Rogers, introduced in 1888
Marlboro: *Warner* by Holmes and Edwards *and* William Rogers and Sons, introduced in 1888
Jacquard Rose: *Rose* by Rogers and Brothers

Since "Warner" was introduced in 1888 by both Holmes and Edwards and in 1847 by Rogers, it is hard to tell who actually developed the pattern.

As a collector, this gives you the advantage of mixing manufacturers to complete a set. The original manufacturers of *Amaranth* and *Perfection* (shown in Figure 5-38) have not been identified.

1880s forward – Matching flatware and hollowware sets begin to appear and are common by the 1890s for both silver and silver-plate.

Flatware patterns are registered in large numbers beginning in the late 19th century and continuing until World War I.

Putting it All Together

A pattern such as *Tipped* is not as hard to date as you might think, although it has been made for almost three hundred years. Earlier you read that the shape of the stem changed over the centuries.

If you find a piece of silver flatware in a pattern that has been made for a long time, you can use the shape of the stem to help date it.

One-piece versus two-piece construction will also help narrow the date range.

If a **silver** spoon or fork is cast, it was made sometime after about 1830.

Different patterns become more available after 1800, but it is not until after the American Civil War that patterns are registered in any great numbers.

As you look over pictures of serving pieces, keep in mind that not all manufacturers made every piece in every pattern. Manufacturers continued to make popular patterns for many years. Often, serving pieces for older patterns were introduced later as new forms developed.

Chapter 6: Silver Styles

Shortly after the first vessel was formed, someone probably got the idea that it would be great if it was both functional *and* attractive; so, the marriage between function and form began.

The style of the piece can help us date it. Combining marks, construction techniques, and style will help you date and attribute your silver.

Scarcity is a Dating Clue

Most of the American antique silver you are likely to come across will not date before the early 19th century. As a young country, our ancestors were more concerned with creating things that gave people basic comforts. As an English colony, we were expected to produce raw materials for British tradesmen. In exchange, we would receive finished goods from England, which included applicable tariffs. (We all remember that nasty tax on tea!)

The British never opened an assay office in the colonies, because we were not supposed to make such things as silver hollowware and flatware. In addition, as you saw in the first chapter, silver was expensive. Most of the significant silver strikes did not occur until the mid 19th century, so silver in colonies was scarce, too. When a silver item went out of style, it was a common practice to melt it down and have it made into something more fashionable, making early pieces that much more scarce.

The majority of English silver that comes up for sale or auction dates back to about the mid 18th century. The English have a hallmarking system that dates back to the 14th century, but all the important silver from this period is in museums and private collections.

The French experienced tremendous political upheaval in the late 18th century that continued throughout most of the 19th century. Silver was melted down to pay for the wars and revolution. The few pieces that remain are in museums and private collections, with some occasionally coming up for sale at auction.

Silversmithing in America only dates back to the mid 17th century.

Few examples pre-date 1750. Styles in America can be as much as 10 years behind styles on the European continent.

If we add to this the fact that all the silver styles have been reproduced, this greatly narrows the dating possibilities for most of the silver you will find.

The examples include style elements from many forms of fine and decorative art. This gives us a sense of how each style so completely dominated the era in which it was popular.

Style Elements

Gothic
(c1150 to c1420)

With the church as the most stable influence in Europe, the Gothic style in decorative arts can be expressed in two words: *miniature cathedrals*. Think of old castles with tracery windows, pointed arches, crockets, trefoils, quatrefoils, linenfold patterns, and heraldic devices like crowns and shields. Look for things you would expect to see in front of an old church.

You will most likely see silver hollowware from this period in museums, but spoons and forks that date back this far are available for sale at auction and on the Internet.

Renaissance
(1420 to c1650)

Renaissance means "rebirth." An interest in ancient Greece and Rome inspired this movement, which began in Italy and then spread to Spain and France. The English were very committed to the Gothic style. The Renaissance style took about one hundred years to catch on in England.

Expect to see acanthus leaves, rinceau borders with scrolling foliage, Greek key borders, animal forms, garlands, and sculptural forms of men and women in flowing robes. Expect to see caryatids and Atlantes figures. These are Greek women and men used as supporting columns. Sometimes only the upper portion of the body is represented, with the lower body forming a column.

Other style elements include putti. These are depictions of children, usually nude. Cherubs have wings. Fantastic animals such as gargoyles and dragons are also found.

Patterns tend to be dense, with a preference for allover, dimensional decorations.

Baroque
(1620 to 1700)

Originally, Baroque meant "irregular" or grotesque. There is a belief that early Baroque was actually late Renaissance, but Baroque is a distinct style which features exaggerated oversized forms with large curves, heavy ornament and all-over decoration. This period is also considered to be "The Golden Age of Silversmiths." The silver styles of this period are massive and bold. Because of this, silversmiths used a heavier gauge for the bodies of their works to maintain proportions. Large acanthus leaves, curving cartouches, and curving dolphins all suggest motion. *Massive* and *motion* would be the best words to describe the Baroque period.

Rococo
(c1695 to 1760)

Rococo is often described as "the feminization of Baroque." As with Baroque, the preference for allover ornament continues, but the scale becomes smaller and less overpowering. In silver we see cut-card work, gadrooned rims, horizontal and vertical straps, and reeding. The acanthus leaf and rinceau foliage are still popular, but the scale is much more delicate. Other style elements are garlands of fruit and flowers, shell motifs, and diaper pattern with dots or florets. Claw and ball feet became popular towards the end of the Rococo period.

Both the Queen Anne style (1702-1760) and the Chippendale style in America (1755–1780) are considered to be subsets of the Rococo style.

Neo-Classical
(c1755 to 1805)

Inspired by excavations of ancient ruins in Italy and Greece, this style of design is popular in the United States from about 1780 to 1820, later than on the European Continent. Expect to see Prince of Wales feathers, Greek key patterns, egg and dart patterns, medallions, shield shapes, drapery, sheaves of wheat, and attributes of music. In the United States, this period is usually called the *Early Federal Period.*

Here in the United States, after about 1800, a variation of the Neo-Classical style, called the *American Director style* became popular. You will also see rosettes, cornucopias, grape clusters, urns with festoons of flowers, laurel wreaths and quarter fan inlay. After about 1804, bowknot motifs, rosettes, lyres, acanthus leaves, plumes, cornucopia, drapery, laurel wreaths and trumpets are also popular.

Empire
(c1799 to 1815)

The Empire style is Neo-Classical in nature, but adds *imperial* forms of ancient Rome, Greece and Egypt. Majestic and graceful birds such as hawks, eagles, and swans are common style elements, suggesting symbols of ancient royalty. With Napoleon's ventures into Egypt, such forms as lotus borders, hieroglyphics, hawks, and sphinxes also become popular.

The Empire period in the United States is later, from about 1820 to 1840.

Late Classicism
1812 to 1830

In England, this style is called the *Regency Style.* In France it is called the *Restauration style,* and in the United States it is called *Late Classicism.* In America, this style is popular from about 1835 to 1850. In general, the decorative styles of the Neo-Classical and Empire periods are still in use, but more emphasis is made on the form itself, with scrolls and curves taking the place of many of the decorative elements. In the United States, decoration is usually done by engraving.

Gothic Revival
(1825 to 1870)

Always looking back for inspiration, Gothic Revival forms become popular by the mid 19th century. As mentioned earlier, the watchwords are "miniature cathedrals." Look for tracery, high arches, trefoils, quatrefoils, linenfold, and rosettes.

Rococo Revival
(1845 to 1920)

This light and flowing style becomes popular again in the mid 19th century and continues into the early 20th century. Around 1900, there was an influx of Dutch Rococo Revival silver that is still common in the market place today. Look for a lot of scrolling foliage (rinceau) floral patterns, gadrooned rims, reeding, and acanthus leaves. Other style elements are garlands of fruit and flowers, shell motifs, and diaper ground with dots or florets.

Renaissance Revival
(1860 to 1885)

The Renaissance Revival style of the 19th century uses motifs and style elements similar to those of the Renaissance period. In addition to figural elements, you should also expect to see acorn motifs and medallions. As with the Renaissance style, expect to see acanthus leaves, rinceau borders with scrolling foliage, Greek key borders, animal forms, and sculptural forms of men and women in flowing robes and garlands. Also expect to see caryatids and Atlantes figures. These are Greek women and men used as supporting columns. Sometimes, only the upper portion of the body is represented, with the lower body forming a column.

Colonial Revival
(1875 to 1945)

Partly inspired by our centennial in 1876, the *Colonial Revival style* copied style elements from what people thought was "colonial." In practice, 17th and 18th style elements were used. This includes things like lyres, bowknots, drapery, and motifs like those in the Neo-Classical period, along with other decorative elements from the early Federal and Empire periods.

Exotic, Nature, and Japanese-Inspired Forms (1875 to 1910)

As European monarchies became less influential on styles, people looked to exotic forms for inspiration. Though Exotic, Nature, and Japanese-Inspired motifs are separate style elements, often you will see these style elements combined in one form. We sometimes refer to this as the Aesthetic style.

In general, naturalistic motifs (inspired by scientific discoveries of the time) show branches, birds, and floral motifs combined in a single piece. With the influence of such Far East countries as Japan and Turkey, expect to see cherry blossoms, fans, cranes, stylized "fringe," and tassel motifs.

Arts and Crafts (1880 to 1920)

Not surprisingly, the 19th century had its critics, too. The industrial revolution was creating machinery that could duplicate the look of hand-made ornamentation. Nearly every surface that could be covered, *was* covered – by machine-made designs. The *Arts and Crafts movement* was a reaction to over-ornamentation. It emphasized one-of-a-kind, handmade items with simple handcrafted designs. In silver, the distinct look of allover hammer marks is characteristic of the Arts and Crafts style. This is a time-consuming technique, so some ingenious manufacturers devised a machine process to imitate hand-hammered marks, too.

Art Nouveau (1885 to 1915)

Art Nouveau, literally "new art," was probably one of the only original styles of the 19th century. Instead of reacting to what was being produced or looking back for inspiration, Art Nouveau did not try to imitate life or nature. Art Nouveau tried to capture the "essence" of life. The Art Nouveau style is often thought of as flowing vines, budding flowers and exotic creatures like dragonflies and bats. Ladies in long, loose gowns with flowing hair are also part of this style, sometimes represented in metamorphosis, or transformational form.

Art Deco
(1917 to 1945)

In 1925 the Paris Exposition, known as the *"Exposition des Arts Decoratifs,"* exhibited new, sleek and modern designs. Today we call this style *"Art Deco,"* but it was not called this until the 1960s. This new style was stripped of tangles of vines and flowers. It used geometric forms and stylized motifs that *suggested* rather than *represented* its style elements. Expect to see geometric patterns and shapes along with speed and motion motifs. Ancient Egypt also had a hand in influencing the styles of this period. When King Tut's tomb was unearthed in 1927, "Tut-mania" took over. You will often see sleek Egyptian motifs blended in with Art Deco. The gazelle also makes an appearance in the Art Deco period. It represented swift, graceful movement.

You can refer to the overall style of a piece, such as Rococo Revival, but if you know the country of origin, you can also include the monarch's name. An English piece made in the Rococo Revival style can also be called Victorian Rococo Revival. A French piece made in the Rococo Revival style can also be referred to as Louis XIV Revival. Since we in the United States were once a British colony, anything made here can be referred to with British monarch's name.

Gothic
(c1150 to c1420)

Figure 6-1: Façade detail, Egliésia de Santa Maria del Mar, Barcelona, Spain, 1329–1384, with tracery, pointed arches, crockets, and trefoils

Figure 6-2: Linen fold on a 14th century coffer, Palace of the Popes, Avignon, France

Figure 6-3: Vatican Coat of Arms, a heraldic device, Palace of the Popes, Avignon, France, 14th century

Renaissance
(1420 to c1650)

Figure 6-5: Perseus beheading Medusa, detail of base with caryatids, scrolls, garlands, and animal forms

Figure 6-4: Perseus beheading Medusa, by Cellini, 1545–1554, Piazza della Signoria, Florence, Italy, taken from Greek mythology

Figure 6-6: Renaissance chalice with rinceau scrolls, Italy, c1500, San Diego Museum of Art

Figure 6-7: Renaissance chalice, detail

Figure 6-8: Façade detail, Palace of the Popes Plaza,
Avignon, France, 1619

Baroque
(1620 to 1700)

Figure 6-9: German tankards,
gilt, with heavy, rinceau
scrolls, 1600–1625, Victoria
and Albert Museum

Figure 6-10: High-back chair,
1686-1693, Victoria and
Albert Museum

Figure 6-11: Below detail of an armchair, 1670, Victoria and Albert Museum; dolphin motif arms, arm supports and handholds

Figure 6-12: Leg detail of an armchair, dolphin motif apron and legs, 1670, Victoria and Albert Museum

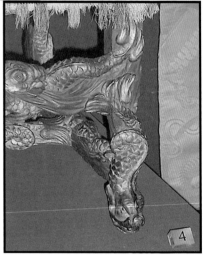

Rococo
(c1695 to 1760)

Figure 6-13: Soup tureen, Sterling, with gadrooned border, scrolling leaves and fruit finial, Victoria and Albert Museum, 1760

Figure 6-14: Gate detail, showing acanthus leaf, shell motif, fronds (palm fronds), and florets, Calvet Museum, Avignon, France, 1753

Figure 6-15: Gate detail, showing acanthus leaf rinceau, florets, and diaper patterning, Calvet Museum, Avignon, France, 1753

Neo-Classical
(c1755 to 1805)

Figure 6-16: Architectural castings reproduced from early Greek and Roman forms, 1755–1830, Victoria and Albert Museum

Empire
(c1799 to 1815)

Figure 6-17: Eight Wallpaper patterns, 1812–1816, showing various Neo-Classical and Empire motifs

Late Classicism
1812 to 1830

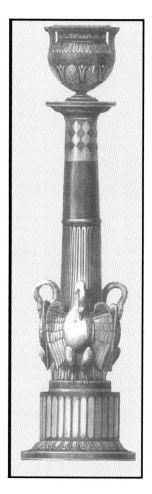

Figure 6-18 (above left): Fireplace panel with Greek key border and classical motifs, from the catalog of the Great Exhibition of 1851

Figure 6-19 (above right): Vase and pedestal with Neo-Classical motifs and borders, from the catalog of the Great Exhibition of 1851

Gothic Revival
(1825 to 1870)

Figure 6-20: Tracery detail from the Great Exhibition of 1851 catalog

Figure 6-21: Crockets and Arches from the Great Exhibition of 1851 catalog

Figure 6-22: Heraldic Devices from the Great Exhibition of 1851 catalog

Figure 6-23: Quatrefoil panel from the 1915-16 Panama-California Exposition

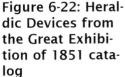

Figure 6-25: Stained glass window framed with Gothic revival framing, 19th century, Vatican Museum, Italy

Figure 6-24: Detail of a drawing for a bracelet, from the catalog of the Great Exhibition of 1851

Rococo Revival
(1845 to 1920)

Figure 6-26: Scrolling foliage (rinceau) reproduced from early Greek and Roman forms, 1755–1830, Victoria and Albert Museum

Figure 6-27: Drinking cup with scrolling foliage, with London Hallmarks for 1855

Figure 6-28: Tea service with diaper pattern on the body, acanthus handles and shell accents, from the catalog of the Great Exhibition of 1851

Figure 6-29: Attributes of music, detail from the catalog of the Paris Exposition of 1867

Renaissance Revival
(1860 to 1885)

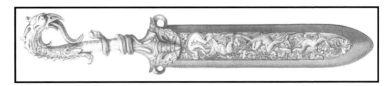

Figure 6-30: Bronze-plated knife with dragon-head, from the catalog of the Paris Exposition of 1867

Figure 6-31: Cutlery and fish knife handles with putti, from the catalog of the Great Exhibition of 1851

Figure 6-32: French Renaissance Revival chalice, 1910 (courtesy of prices4antiques.com)

Colonial Revival
(1875 to 1945)

Figure 6-33: Gorham sterling pitcher and salver exhibited at the Centennial Exposition, 1876

Figure 6-34: Mantle clock, exhibited by the American Clock Company at the Centennial Exposition, 1876

Figure 6-35: The Bryant Vase, exhibited by Tiffany and Company at the Centennial Exposition, 1876

Exotic, Nature, and Japanese-Inspired Forms
(1875 to 1910)

Figure 6-36: Silverplated set by Reed and Barton, exhibited at the Centennial exposition, 1876, and presented to the Emperor of Japan

Figure 6-37: Silverplated tea set, Aesthetic style, fancy goods catalog detail, 1889

Arts and Crafts
(1880 to 1920)

Figure 6-38: Arts and Crafts drinking cup by Liberty and Company, c1900, Eldred's Auction (photo courtesy of prices4antiques.com)

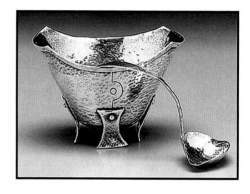

Figure 6-39: American Arts and Crafts sauce boat, c1900 (photo courtesy of prices4antiques.com)

Art Nouveau
(1885 to 1915)

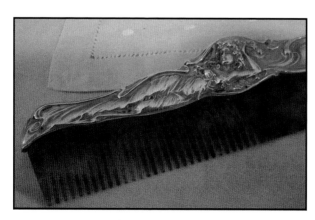

Figure 6-40: Art Nouveau comb, Sterling and tortoise, c1900 (collection of Susan O'Neal)

Figure 6-41: Statuary Detail, 1888, Ciutadella Park, Barcelona, Spain

Figure 6-42: Art Nouveau building façade, c1900, Barcelona, Spain

Art Deco
(1917 to 1945)

Figure 6-43: Butter knife, Sterling handle in the shape of an airplane body (collection of Susan O'Neal)

Figure 6-44: Art Deco architecture, 1930s, Miami, Florida

Art Deco Architecture, and Building Interior Doors, Miami, Florida, 1930's

Chapter 7: Marks on Silver

Most countries have some sort of system for making sure that the content of the silver is represented truthfully. Not only do different countries have different ways of marking silver, but most countries' systems changed over the centuries. Some countries enforced silver marking laws and some did not.

The result is that we can use marks on silver to help us date a piece of silver.

In a feudal society, many early silver marks were based on the arms of the city. If you know the coat of arms used by a particular city, you may be well on the way to identifying your silver. This is not always the most accurate way to *date* a piece of silver, however, because most of the European city arms are quite ancient – most of them were adopted over 600 hundred years ago. The idea is to put all the information together with the silver marks to identify and date silver.

Although this is not intended to be a history lesson, historical events affected the marks each country used to mark silver. This chapter is a summary of that history, along with the changes in the way silver has been marked for hundreds of years.

America - *see the United States*

Australia

Most silver items are imported from England. As with the American colonies, no official hallmarking laws were enacted. The small amount produced in Australia is marked using a numbered system, for example, .925.

Austrian Empire

1200s to 1806 – Austria is a kind of crossroads in Europe, sharing borders with many countries. Influenced by the Habsburgs since the 13th century, the Austrian Empire ruled Austria, Hungary,

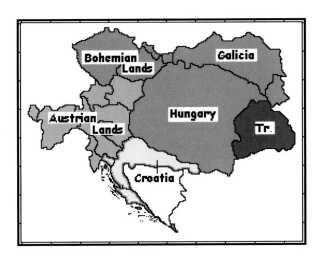

Figure 7-1: Map of the Austrian Empire

Croatia, Galicia, Madrid, Spanish colonies in the Americas, and the Philippines. The Habsburg dynasty, part of the Holy Roman Empire, existed from 1556 to 1806. Most marks in this period use the Habsburg crowned eagle with spread wings.

Austria-Hungary
(1806 to 1918)

1810 – Defeated by Napoleon in 1806, the Austrian Empire was divided into three distinct groups. Each had a different standard for silver.

The German-Slavonian lands (Slavonia) had two standards for silver:
>15 löthige, or .9375 fineness
>13 löthige, or .8125 fineness

The Lombardo-Venetian Kingdom, part of modern-day northern Italy, which included Milan and Venice, had two standards for silver:

>15 löthige, or .9375 fineness
>12 löthige, or .750 fineness

In most cases, the mark was a half-circle. Inside the half-circle was a city letter. "A" was the city letter for Vienna. Below that was the number of löthige, typically 13 enclosed in a circle or other symbol. The year, expressed in four numbers, surrounded the circle.

Figure 7-2: Austro-Hungarian silver mark

The Hungarian Kingdom with Dalmatia, Krakow, and the military frontier had no laws or restrictions for silver standards.

1886 to 1925 – A law was passed that set the same standard for all three regions. Under the new law, four standards were set for silver, using the head of the goddess Diana with a crescent moon. The standard is indicated by the shape of the cartouche and the numeral inside. As in the previous system, the letter indicates the city letter with the letter "A" for Vienna. The name of the manufacturer had to be stamped on all goods.

Figure 7-3: Austro-Hungarian fineness marks, 1886 - 1925

Small items had two standards, .800 fineness represented by a greyhound's head facing right and .750 fineness represented by a lion's head facing left, both enclosed in polygons.

Austria, 1918 to Present

1925 – Beginning on August 23, 1925, silverware carried the maker's mark, the hallmark, and the number indicating the fineness. The hallmarks were changed from the head of the goddess Diana to bird heads.

Figure 7-4: Austrian fineness marks, 1925 forward

Austrian Silver Marks 1925+			
1st Standard .935	2nd Standard .900	3rd Standard .835	4th Standard .800

1954 – The first standard was reduced to .925 fineness.

Belgium

1795 to 1814 – Belgium was under the occupation of the French. Refer to Figures 7-20 and 7-21 for hallmarks. Belgium would have used the silver marks listed for the French departments (provinces), with two standards for silver, .950 and .800. The maker's mark was also required.

1814 to 1831 – Under Dutch occupation, the standards for silver and their marks changed. The first standard was set at .934 fineness using the number "1" above crossed laurel branches. The figures are enclosed in a rectangle with cut corners. The second standard was set at .833. The symbol is the number "2" above crossed laurel branches, enclosed in a square. (See Figure 7-5.)

Silver items were also stamped with a guarantee mark. Large items were stamped with a hand holding a baton, enclosed in a circle. Small items received a guarantee stamp in the shape of an urn with a single laurel branch inside. Above the hand was a letter for the city of assay. Below is a partial city list. The maker's mark was also required.

A = Brussels, B = Antwerp, C = Gand, D = Liège, E = Mons.

1832 to 1868 – During this period the first standard of .933 fineness was represented by a lyre above the number "1" and the letter "T." A double-faced figure with the number "2" above it indicated the second standard of .800 fineness.

The head of Minerva was used as the assay guarantee mark for large items.

Small items were not required to carry the assay office mark. A dagger was used to indicate the fineness of .833. Figure 7-6 shows the marks for this period.

The maker's mark was also required.

1868 to 1942 – The manufacture of precious metal ware was permitted in any standard. Compulsory marking stopped, but buyers and sellers could have precious metal tested and stamped at the testing office. The office tested for two silver standards: .900 fineness and .800 fineness.

For the first silver standard of .900, the stamp was the letter "A" for "argent" (silver), and the number "1" enclosed in a triangle with cut corners. For the second standard of .800, the letter "A" and number "2" were enclosed in a square with cut corners. Small versions of each mark were used for small items. Assay office guarantee marks were no longer required. (See Figure 7-7.)

1942 to present – The Belgian government set a minimum fineness requirement of .500 for silver. Although not required, items could be submitted for official hallmarking for buyers or sellers who wanted an official assay. Only two standards could be submitted for assay, .925 and .835 fineness. The assay mark for the first standard of .925 was a four-petal flower with a "1" in the center. The second standard of .835 used the same flower enclosed in a square with the Roman numeral "II" in the center (Figure 7-8).

The maker's mark must appear in relief, enclosed in a barrel-shaped cartouche.

The fineness mark is the letter "A" (argent) followed by the fineness expressed in thousandths. Alternatively, the letter "A" could be enclosed in a separate oval (Figure 7-8).

Figure 7-5: Belgian assay and fineness marks, 1814 to 1831

Figure 7-6: Belgian assay and fineness marks, 1832 to 1869

Figure 7-7: Belgian fineness marks, 1869 to 1942

Figure 7-8: Belgian official marks, 1942 to present

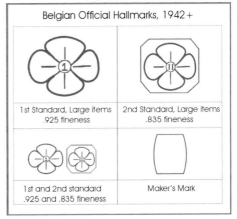

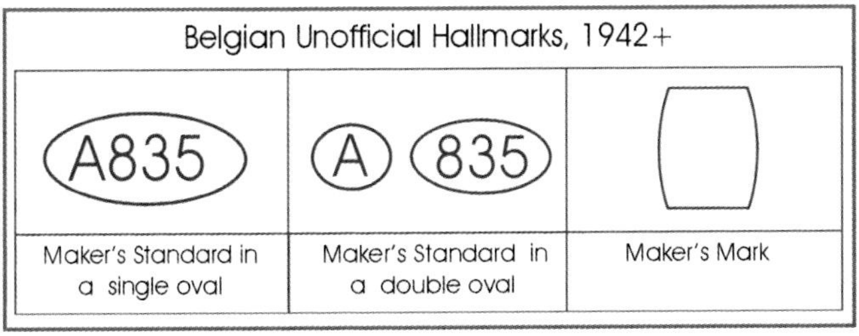

Figure 7-9: Belgian maker's mark and fineness, 1942 to present

Britain – *see United Kingdom*

Canada

During the early part of her history (between 1700 and 1763), Canada used marks similar to those of the French system, using either a crown, fleur-de-lis, or star above the initials of the maker, all within a simple cartouche.

As the English exerted more influence towards the late eighteenth century, Canadian silversmiths began using just their initials, either in italics or in Roman letters surrounded by a simple rectangle or cartouche. Some silversmiths in the Montreal or Quebec provinces added the words "Montreal" or "Quebec."

At the beginning of the nineteenth century, Canadian marks began to look more like English hallmarks. In some cases, they copied official hallmarks and duty marks.

Silversmiths in other provinces began adding the initials of their provinces enclosed in rectangles or ovals. H, HX or XNS was used for Halifax (Nova Scotia). St. J or NB was used for St. John (New Brunswick).

The Canadian Act, effective March 13, 1908, stated that silverware must be .925 fineness. A lion's head inside the letter "C" was used to indicate that the object had been certified as .925 fineness. This was the National Mark of Canada from 1937 to 1978. On July 1, 1978, the mark was changed to a maple leaf surrounded by the letter "C." Both are show in Figure 7-10.

In 1898, the Montreal firm of Henry Birks and Sons began using a marking system that looked a lot like the English hall marking system.

| Canadian National Mark 1908 to 1978 | Canadian National Mark 1978+ |

Figure 7-10: Canadian national marks

China

During the Chi'ing dynasty (1844 to 1912), Chinese silver became a popular export item, with many Chinese silver pieces sent to the United States.

Many Chinese silversmiths used English letters with or without Chinese characters as their marks. Many used English pseudo-marks, so you may find Chinese ideograms along with a cat or a lion stamped on the piece.

108

China did not regulate the silver content of their wares. Export silver can be .800 fineness, with many examples over .925.

Denmark

1685 to 1893 – In Denmark, the basic unit of measurement for silver is the loth (.0625 fineness). On November 7, 1685, the king of Denmark ordained that silver must worked to a standard of at least 13½ loth .844 fineness with a tolerance of ½ loth (a minimum of .812 fineness). The king further required that silver goods be marked with the manufacturer's stamp.

A warden would assay the item and mark it with the arms of the city if the piece was of the required fineness. Most of the silver was made and assayed in Copenhagen, represented by three towers (Figure 7-11).

The warden also marked the piece with his own initials. In practice, many of the city marks from this period included either two- or four-digit year marks.

The signs of the zodiac were used to indicate the month of assay. They are shown in the section on Norwegian hallmarks (See Norway, Figures 7-58 and 7-59).

The easiest way to date silver from this period is by identifying the warden who marked the silver, as shown below. Keep in mind that sometimes the wardens used only one initial.

1677 to 1904 – Danish Warden Marks

> C. Ludolf: 1677 to 1729
> P. N. v. Haven: 1729 to 1749
> C. Fabricius: 1749 to 1787
> F. Fabricius: 1787 to 1823
> C. P. Naebo: 1823 to 1827
> J. G. G. Fabricius: 1827 to 1831
> C. O. Moller: 1831 to 1840
> P. R. Hinnerup: 1840 to 1863
> S. Groth: 1863 to 1904

1893 to present – The guarantee mark was simplified. Instead of using a different mark for each city, the Copenhagen

Three-Tower mark was used as the control mark for all cities. The mark was modified, showing the last two digits of the year represented in wavy lines under the towers.

Figure 7-11: Copenhagen fineness guarantee mark, 1685 to 1893

Figure 7-12: Danish control mark with year digits

Egypt

1916 to present – Egypt adopted a formal hallmarking system. Since September 1, 1916, Egyptian silver must show three marks: the fineness, an official mark, and a date letter (A = 1916, B = 1917, etc.).

Figure 7-13: Egyptian marks for Cairo, Alexandria, Tanta and Beni Suef with official marks and date letters

Egyptian Marks on Silver

Marks	Cairo	Alexandria	Tanta	Beni Suef
.900 fine				
.800 fine				
.600 fine				
Official Mark until 1946				
Official Mark after 1946				
Date Letter before 1946	 N	 N	 N	 N
Date Letter after 1946				

Roman letters were used until 1946, Arabic letters after 1946, as shown. The date letter changed in May of each year, so one 12 month period covers two calendar years.

England – *see United Kingdom*

Finland

1154 to 1759 – Finland had an association with Sweden for almost 700 years. Under the rule of Sweden's King Erik, the earliest mark consisted of a zigzag line where the doyen of the town scraped away some of the metal for testing.

1759 to 1809 – During this period, Finland used the mark of the Swedish Government, three crowns enclosed in a tri-lobed cartouche (Figure 7-14), along with the *Swedish* date letter (see Figure 7-92 in Sweden). It is assumed that Finland had the same minimum requirements for silver as Sweden, .830 fineness.

1810 to 1929 – In 1808 Finland was conquered by Russia and remained a Grand Duchy under the Russian Empire until shortly after the Bolshevik Revolution in 1917.

During this time, Finland established its own assay mark, a crown in a heart-shaped cartouche (Figure 7-15), a fineness mark (Figure 7-16) a date letter (Figure 7-17) and a city mark (Figure 7-18). The date-letter codes they used were similar to codes used in the Swedish system. The maker's mark was also required.

Finland used *lods* to measure silver, .813 lod = .830 fineness. During this period they also used Russian *zolotniks* to show fineness. 84 zolotniks = .875 fineness.

A series of locality marks (city marks) was mandatory until 1943. Today locality marks are optional. A partial list is provided in Figure 7-18.

Figure 7-14: Swedish 3-crown mark used in Finland

Figure 7-15: Finnish assay mark

Figure 7-16: Finish fineness mark

Figure 7-17: Finnish date-letter codes

Finnish Date Letters 1810 - 1999

Code	Year	Code	Year	Code	Year	Code	Year	Code	Year	Code	Year	Code	Year	Code	Year
A	1810	A2	1834	A3	1858	A4	1882	A5	1906	A6	1930	A7	1954	A8	1976
B	1811	B2	1835	B3	1859	B4	1883	B5	1907	B6	1931	B7	1955	B8	1977
C	1812	C2	1836	C3	1860	C4	1884	C5	1908	C6	1932	C7	1956	C8	1978
D	1813	D2	1837	D3	1861	D4	1885	D5	1909	D6	1933	D7	1957	D8	1979
E	1814	E2	1838	E3	1862	E4	1886	E5	1910	E6	1934	E7	1958	E8	1980
F	1815	F2	1839	F3	1863	F4	1887	F5	1911	F6	1935	F7	1959	F8	1981
G	1816	G2	1840	G3	1864	G4	1888	G5	1912	G6	1936	G7	1960	G8	1982
H	1817	H2	1841	H3	1865	H4	1889	H5	1913	H6	1937	H7	1961	H8	1983
I	1818	I2	1842	I3	1866	I4	1890	I5	1914	I6	1938	I7	1962	I8	1984
K	1819	K2	1843	K3	1867	K4	1891	K5	1915	K6	1939	K7	1963	K8	1985
L	1820	L2	1844	L3	1868	L4	1892	L5	1916	L6	1940	L7	1964	L8	1986
M	1821	M2	1845	M3	1869	M4	1893	M5	1917	M6	1941	M7	1965	M8	1987
N	1822	N2	1846	N3	1870	N4	1894	N5	1918	N6	1942	N7	1966	N8	1988
O	1823	O2	1847	O3	1871	O4	1895	O5	1919	O6	1943	O7	1967	O8	1989
P	1824	P2	1848	P3	1872	P4	1896	P5	1920	P6	1944	P7	1968	P8	1990
Q	1825	Q2	1849	Q3	1873	Q4	1897	Q5	1921	Q6	1945	Q7	1969	Q8	1991
R	1826	R2	1859	R3	1874	R4	1898	R5	1922	R6	1946	R7	1970	R8	1992
S	1827	S2	1851	S3	1875	S4	1899	S5	1923	S6	1947	S7	1971	S8	1993
T	1828	T2	1852	T3	1876	T4	1900	T5	1924	T6	1948	T7	1972	T8	1994
U	1829	U2	1853	U3	1877	U4	1901	U5	1925	U6	1949	U7	1973	U8	1995
V	1830	V2	1854	V3	1878	V4	1902	V5	1926	V6	1950	V7	1974	V8	1996
X	1831	X2	1855	X3	1879	X4	1903	X5	1927	X6	1951	X7	1975	X8	1997
Y	1832	Y2	1856	Y3	1880	Y4	1904	Y5	1928	Y6	1952	Y7	1976	Y8	1998
Z	1833	Z2	1857	Z3	1881	Z4	1905	Z5	1929	Z6	1953	Z7	1977	Z8	1999

Figure 7-18: Finnish city marks

Currently, the minimum fineness is .800, expressed in thousandths.

Figure 7-19: Finnish fineness marks, expressed in thousandths

France

In the 18ᵗʰ century, kings and princes melted down much of France's silver to pay for their extravagant lifestyles. During the French Revolution in 1789, more silver hollowware and flatware was melted down to finance the war. The result is that very little French silver dating before the nineteenth century exists outside of museums and private collections. Our overview of early French silver laws provides a background to help understand the variation in French marks that you may find in your search for antique silver.

History of French Silver Fineness

As early as 1258, France required that all silver be of the Sterling standard, or .925 fineness. In 1378, Charles V set the standard at 11 deniers and 12 grains (.957 fineness). The silversmith was allowed a tolerance of 2 grains (0.00694). This standard applied mainly to Paris silversmiths, as many French provinces were not under the rule of the French king at that time.

By 1554, such French provinces as Lorraine, Franche-Comté, Flanders, Rousillon, Béarn, Flanders Hainault, and Alsace were brought under crown rule but were exempt from duty marks. These provinces continued to use standards lower than .957. The fineness ranged from .730 to .948. Avignon belonged to the French Papacy, which had its own regulations.

In 1783, a law was passed to regulate silver fineness at .957. In 1791 during the French Revolution and afterwards during "The Reign of Terror," silver marking laws were suspended.

It was not until November 1797 that the standard of silver fineness was re-established. At this time, two standards for silver came into use. This first standard was .950 fineness. The second standard was set at .800 fineness. This dual standard remains in effect today.

Finally, in 1972, the first standard that had been set at .950 fineness was returned to .925, the same as it had been seven hundred years earlier!

Marks on French Silver Before the French Revolution

Before the French revolution, a piece of French silver would carry at least four marks: The maker's mark, the guarantee mark, the charge mark, and the discharge mark.

The Maker's Mark

The maker's mark is probably the most consistent mark used in the French system of hallmarking. An edict of Philippe le Hardi in 1275 required the use of the maker's mark on French silver. It consisted of the initials of the maker.

In addition to using initials, sometimes the maker added a device that might symbolize the maker's name. Jacques Delavigne used a vine leaf, Louis Regnard used a fox, J. P. Marteau used a hammer, and Jean du Moulin used a windmill.

Sometime near the end of the fifteenth century, two dots over the initials are supposed to have been added, believed to represent the tolerance of 2 grains mentioned earlier.

The Guarantee Mark

Before the Revolution, the earliest French hallmarks used either a crown or fleur-de-lis in combination with the letter for the town of assay. Later, the crown was used with the fleur-de-lis. It was called the *poinçon de contremarque*. It was placed above the maker's mark with both the guarantee mark and the maker's mark encircled in a small cartouche.

The Warden of the goldsmith's guild would place the guarantee mark on the piece.

Figure 7-20: Maker's mark with the *poinçon de contremarque* (guarantee mark)

Charge and Discharge Marks

In the 17th century, a set of duty marks came into use, called charge and discharge marks. A special tax farmer was used to place the charge and discharge marks.

At first, only the charge mark was used to show payment of the tax. In 1672, the charge mark was used register the unfinished piece. The town mark or town letter with a crown above it was used as the charge mark. *After* the piece was registered and marked, the maker could take the piece back to the Warden to receive the guarantee mark.

The town letters are as follows:

Paris	A	Bordeaux	K	Nantes	T
Rouen	B	Bayonne	L	Troyes	V
Caen	C	Marseilles	M	Lille	W
Lyon	D	Toulouse	M	Amiens	X
Tours	E	Montpellier	N	Bourges	Y
Angers	F	Riom	O	Grenoble	Z
Poitiers	G	Dijon	P	Aix	&
La Rochelle	H	Perpignan	Q	Metz	AA
Limoges	I	Orléans	R	Strasbourg	BB
Limoges	J	Reims	S	Besançon	C

The arms of the town or its initials were often used in the provinces. Sometimes this mark was combined with the Warden's mark (the guarantee mark).

The discharge mark was used to show that the duty was paid on the piece. At first, there were no special discharge marks. They could be an animal, an animal head, body parts, leaves, or birds. It was very confusing. Each town used a different mark and changed it every two to seven years. There was no set system for the type of marks used for discharge marks.

In 1783, Louis XVI decreed that each town would have one mark that did not change. Figure 7-21 shows charge and discharge marks for the major French cities. They were in use from 1784 to 1791.

Punches in Use for Silver from 1784 until 1791						
Mint Towns	**Charge**		**Discharge**		**General Punches**	
	Large Silver Works	Small Silver Works	Large Silver Works	Small Silver Works	Distinction	Types
Paris					Ingots for drawing	
Lyon					Foreign Plate	
Bordeaux					Ancient Works	
Rouen					Very Small Works	

Figure 7-21: Charge and discharge marks in use from 1784 to 1791

Date Marks

In 1472, France began to use date letters. They consisted of a letter for the year with a crown above it. The date letters changed with the election of the Wardens. From 1661 forward, the elections were held in July or August. The letters "J," "U" and "W" were omitted until 1783, when the letter "U" was added to the system. From 1784 until 1789, a crowned "P" was used with the last two digits of the year. Following is a list of eighteenth century date letters with an example of the years 1788 and 1789.

French Date Marks:

1697 to 1704: C, D, E, F, G, H, I, K
1704 to 1711: K, L, M, N, O, P, Q, R
1711 to 1713: S, T, V
1714 to 1717: X, Y, Z
1717 to 1722: A, B, C, D, E
1722 to 1727: E, F, G, H, I, K, L
1727 to 1732: L, M, N, O, P, Q
1732 to 1738: Q, R, S, T, V, X, Y
1738 to 1744: Y, Z, A, B, C, D
1744 to 1750: D, E, F, G, H, I, K
1750 to 1756: K, L, M, N, O, P, Q
1756 to 1762: Q, R, S, T, V, X, Y
1762 to 1768: Y, Z, A, B, C, D, E
1768 to 1775: E, F, G, H, I, K, L, M
1775 to 1781: M, N, O, P, Q, R
1781 to 1783: R, S, T
1783 to 1789: T, U, then P84 to P89

Figure 7-22: 1788 and 1789 French crowned letter "P" and year digits

Import Marks

A different series of marks were used for imported and exported silver. Look for the letters "E. T." or "E." The letter(s) stand for *étrange* (stranger).

Marks on French Silver after the French Revolution

French Marks in Use from November 19, 1797 to September 1, 1809

On November 19, 1797, a new system of marking was adopted in France. This system applied to all of France, not just Paris and a few provinces. These marks formed the foundation for all later legislation.

The new system had five marks: the standard mark, the assay mark, the maker's mark, the verification mark, and the import mark.

Figure 7-23 shows the punches used from November 17, 1797 to September 1, 1809, including the standard mark, assay marks, foreign marks and verification marks.

The standard mark. Giving in to pressures of international commerce, two standards were set for silver, .950 fineness and .800 fineness. A Gaelic cock was used for the both standards, but the number "1" was used for the first standard and the number "2" was used for the second standard. The location of the number was in front of the rooster for Paris and behind the rooster for the departments (provinces). The rooster stands upright in the first standard and is walking in the second standard.

The assay mark. Assay marks were divided into three sizes: large, medium, and small. The head of a Greek philosopher is used for both large and medium items. The surrounding shield is oval-shaped for large items and round for medium-sized items. The figure has an "8" and a "5" next to the ears for Paris, but nothing for the departments. The small assay mark is a hatchet for both Paris and the departments.

There were special assay marks for silver ingots and silver wire, as shown in Figure 7-23.

The verification mark. It was decided that any item marked before the new system took effect would simply be *verified* for content. It was called the *poinçon de recense*. The mark was the profile of a man wearing a kind of turban surrounded by an oval for Paris, with an outline of the profile for the departments. The only difference between the stamp for large and small items was the size of the stamp.

The import mark. Foreign items were not tested. They were marked with the head of Hermes, flanked by the letters "E" and "T." Small foreign items were marked with a capital "E."

Watch marks. The city of Besançon had long been known for watchmaking. At this time, special marks were introduced for watches made in Besançon, as shown in Figure 7-23.

The maker's mark. A kind of a flattened diamond called a "lozenge" was used for the maker's mark. The maker's initials were placed inside the lozenge. This symbol with initials is still used to identify the maker. (See Figure 7-24.)

Figure 7-23: French hallmarks in use from 1797 to 1809

Table of French Punches in use from November 19, 1797 to September 1, 1809

Distinction	Paris	Departments	Distinction	Paris	Departments
Silver 1st Standard 0.950			Large Silver Assay		
Silver 2nd Standard 0.800			Medium Silver Assay		
Foreign Large Items			Small Silver Assay		
Foreign Small Items			Silver Ingots Assay		
Watches made at Besançon Large Items			Silver Wire Assay		
Watches made at Besançon Small Items			Large Recense (Verification) of previous marks		
Lozenge shape for the maker's mark			Small Recense (Verification) of previous marks		

119

 **Figure 7-24: Lozenge shape for the maker's mark**

French Marks in Use from September 1, 1809 to August 16, 1819

On September 1, 1809, new marking laws went into effect. Special marks for watches, ingots, and wire were no longer required.

The basic system using two silver standards remained, and Paris used different symbols from those of departments. We still have five marks: the standard mark, the assay mark, the maker's mark, the verification mark, and the import mark.

Figure 7-25 shows the symbols in use from September 1, 1809 to August 16, 1819.

French Marks in Use from August 16, 1819, to May 10, 1838

On August 16, 1819 the marking system was again modified. The basic system using two silver standards remained and Paris still used different symbols than departments. We still have five marks (the standard mark, the assay mark, the maker's mark, the verification mark and the import mark), but the appearance of the marks changed again. The assay for watches was brought back with a new symbol. Figure 7-26 shows the table of punches in use from August 16, 1819 to May 10, 1838.

The departments were separated into nine divisions. Nine *divisional punches* were introduced (Figure 7-27). There were between nine and fourteen assay offices in each department. Each assay office was assigned a number for large works. The number flanked the head of an ancient nobleman wearing a wreath.

Each assay office used divisional punches for small assay items, as shown in Figure 7-27. A letter, a cross, or the number 8 identified the individual office within the division.

Divisional punches were used with the verification marks, too. Large items were marked with a hound and an assay office number. Small verification items were marked the same way as small assay items, using the same divisional punch and identification system.

Figure 7-25: French hallmarks in use from 1809 to 1819

Table of French Punches in use from September 1, 1809 to August 16, 1819

Distinction	Paris	Departments	Distinction	Paris	Departments
Silver 1st Standard 0.950			Large Silver Assay		
Silver 2nd Standard 0.800			Medium Silver Assay		
Foreign Large Items			Small Silver Assay		
Foreign Small Items			Large Recense (Verification) of previous marks		
Lozenge shape for the maker's mark			Medium Recense (Verification) of previous marks	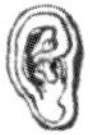	
			Small Recense (Verification) of previous marks		

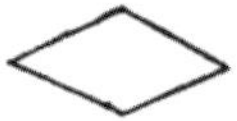

Figure 7-26: French hallmarks in use from 1819 to 1838

Table of French Punches in use from August 16, 1819 to May 10, 1838

Distinction	Paris	Departments	Distinction	Paris	Departments
Silver 1st Standard 0.950			Large Silver Assay		
Silver 2nd Standard 0.800			Medium Silver Assay		None for the Departments
Foreign Large Items			Small Silver Assay		See the Table of Divisional Punches
Foreign Small Items			Large Recense (Verification) of previous marks		See the Table of Divisional Punches
Lozenge shape for the maker's mark			Small Recense (Verification) of previous marks		
Each Bureaux within the Department is assigned a number. In the large silver assay mark for the departments, 84 represents Auxerre. The number 23 shown for the watch assay represents Besançon.			Special Assay for Watches (See the Table of Divisional Punches)		

122

Figure 7-27: French divisional punches in use from 1819 to 1838

Table of French Divisional Punches in use from August 16, 1819 to May 10, 1838

Division	Silver Assay		Verification
North	Butterfly	 Coffee-pot	
North East	Tortoise	 Tower	
East	Shell	 Ciborium	
South East	Beetle	 Goblet	
South	Lysse	 Bell	
South West	Frog	 Watering-pot	
West	Snail	 Ewer	
North West	Thornback	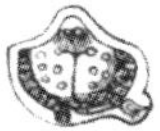 Guitar	
Center	Guinea Pig	 Book	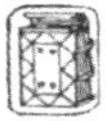

French Marks in Use from May 10, 1838 to Present

A final set of marks was introduced in 1838 and remains in effect today with very minor changes.

The basic system using two silver standards remained and Paris still used different symbols than the departments. We still have the five basic marks (the standard mark, the assay mark, the maker's mark, the verification mark, and the import mark). Figure 7-28 shows the table of French punches in use from 1838 until 1962.

This time, the head of the Roman goddess Minerva identifies silver. The first standard of .950 fineness is shown with the number "1" by her forehead. The second standard of .800 fineness is shown with the number "2" by her chin. Both Paris and the departments used Minerva.

To identify the departments, a symbol was used along with the number. The symbol was placed under her chin for the first standard and by her forehead for the second standard. The symbols used by the departments were letters, astronomy symbols, and Greek letters.

When you see Minerva with both a number and a symbol, you know it was stamped in one of the provinces (departments). When you see the head of Minerva with just a number, you know it was stamped in Paris.

In 1973, the French government changed the double silver standards of .950 and .800. From this point forward, a standard of .925 was introduced. The number one indicates the standard of .925 and is located at the *back* of Minerva's head (versus in front of Minerva's head before 1973). A letter under the chin indicates the decade beginning in 1973. The date letter for 1973 to 1982 is "A." The date letter for 1983 to 1992 is "B."

French Assay Marks in Use from 1838 to Present

From 1797 until 1838, three sizes of assay marks were used. In 1838, the system was simplified using the boar's head for Paris assay and the crab for the departments, each along with the symbol for the individual assay office already in use.

124

In 1962 the "Wild Boar's Head" mark that Paris used for its assay mark was replaced by the "Crab" mark already in use for the departments. The only difference was that Paris did not use a divisional mark.

Foreign Marks in Use from 1838

French import marks. Foreign items are marked with the letters "ET" in a rectangle. They were marked with the weevil if they met the minimum of .800 fineness. The weevil mark was used until 1893.

French export mark in use from July 11, 1840 to April 1, 1879. With political stability returning to the country, France developed a series of export marks to encourage trade with other countries. Export marks were struck free of charge.

For large items, Hermes was surrounded by an octagon and shown with no enclosure for small items.

French export marks in use from April 1, 1879 to August 8, 1973. Still using the head of Hermes, export marks for large items were guaranteed with two standards. The number "1" by the chin indicated the first standard of .950 fineness. The number "2" by the chin indicated the second standard of .800 fineness for large articles. The shapes of the enclosures were the same shapes used for the first and second silver standards already in use for items not intended for export.

For smaller items, a smaller head of Hermes was surrounded by an oval.

French export marks in use since 1973. As with the change in the mark for Minerva, the French government changed the double silver standard of .950 and .800 in 1973. From this point forward, a standard of .925 was introduced. The number "1" indicates the standard of .925. A letter under the chin indicates the decade beginning in 1973. The date letter for 1973 to 1982 is "A." The date letter for 1983 to 1992 is "B."

Figure 7-28: French Standard Marks from 1838 to the 1962

Table of French Punches in use from May 10, 1838 to January 1, 1962

Distinction	Paris and	Departments
Silver 1st Standard 0.950		Department symbol under the chin
Silver 2nd Standard 0.800		Department symbol before the forehead
Foreign Guarantee of 0.800 for large Items	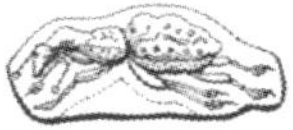	Department symbol between the legs
Foreign Guarantee of 0.800 for small Items		Department symbol between the legs
Foreign Item Mark	E T	
Lozenge shape for the maker's mark	 ◇	

Distinction	Paris	Departments
Silver Assay		 Department symbol between the claws*
Large Recense (Verification) of previous marks		Department symbol below the lower jaw
Small Recense (Verification) of previous marks		Department symbol on the collar
Assay for imported watches 0.800 (A smaller symbol was used for small watches)		Department symbol between the wings and back

*The dotted lines shown by the guarantee marks, the verification mark and the watch assay mark indicate the shape of the punches for the Paris Assay Office only. Each department has a different symbol which is placed in the area of the dotted lines.

**Figure 7-29: 1972 French
.925 silver hallmark**

Large   Small

**Figure 7-30: Hermes export
marks, 1840 to 1879**

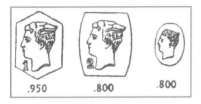

**Figure 7-31: Hermes export
marks, 1879 to 1973**

**Figure 7-32:
Hermes export
mark since 1973**

Germany

The Congress of Vienna simplified the political divisions in Germany, creating 35 monarchies and 4 free cities. These divisions remained unchanged until 1866.

Each state within the German Confederation had its own regulations (or lack of them) for marking silver, but the basic unit of measure was the *loth*, equivalent to 0.0625 fineness, with fine silver containing 16 löthige.

> 16 löthige = 1.00 fineness (pure silver)
> 15 löthige = 0.9375 fineness
> 14 löthige = 0.875 fineness
> 13 löthige = 0.8125 fineness
> 12 löthige = 0.750 fineness

Silver marking was not strictly observed in many of the states. Most cities used simplified forms of the city arms to mark silver. A few cities – namely Augsburg, Dresden, Hanover, and Nurnburg – used date letters, most commonly from the 17th century forward.

Fineness marking was infrequent until the 18th century. Since the majority of the city arms originated between the 10th and 15th centuries, this should give some help in dating pieces that have date letters and fineness shown in löthiges.

Figure 7-33, 7-34, 7-35 and 7-36 shows representations of the city arms for many German cities.

Some towns used portions of the city arms. Hanover usually showed only the small trefoil shown in the city arms.

The German states were unified in 1871. In 1888, new laws took effect for marking silver. The maker's mark had to be registered at the *Reichspatentamt* (Realm patent office). The maker's initials, along with the fineness in numbers, had to be struck on the item by the manufacturer. If the fineness was .800 or greater, the German crown and crescent moon had to be added.

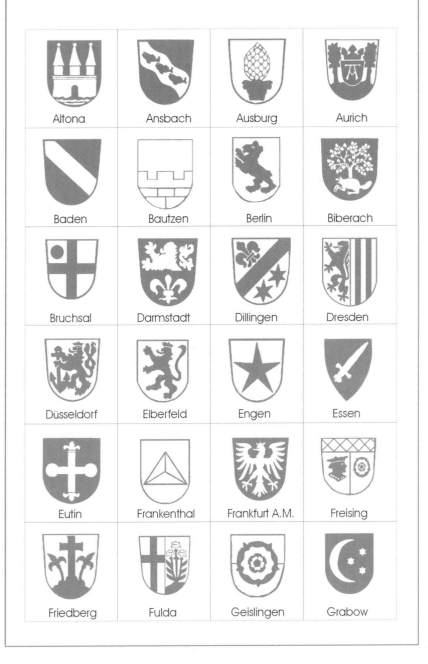

German City Arms used as Silver Marks

Altona	Ansbach	Ausburg	Aurich
Baden	Bautzen	Berlin	Biberach
Bruchsal	Darmstadt	Dillingen	Dresden
Düsseldorf	Elberfeld	Engen	Essen
Eutin	Frankenthal	Frankfurt A.M.	Freising
Friedberg	Fulda	Geislingen	Grabow

Figure 7-33: German City Arms used as Silver Marks, A to G

Figure 7-34: German City Arms used as Silver Marks, G to M

Figure 7-35: German City Arms used as Silver Marks, N to U

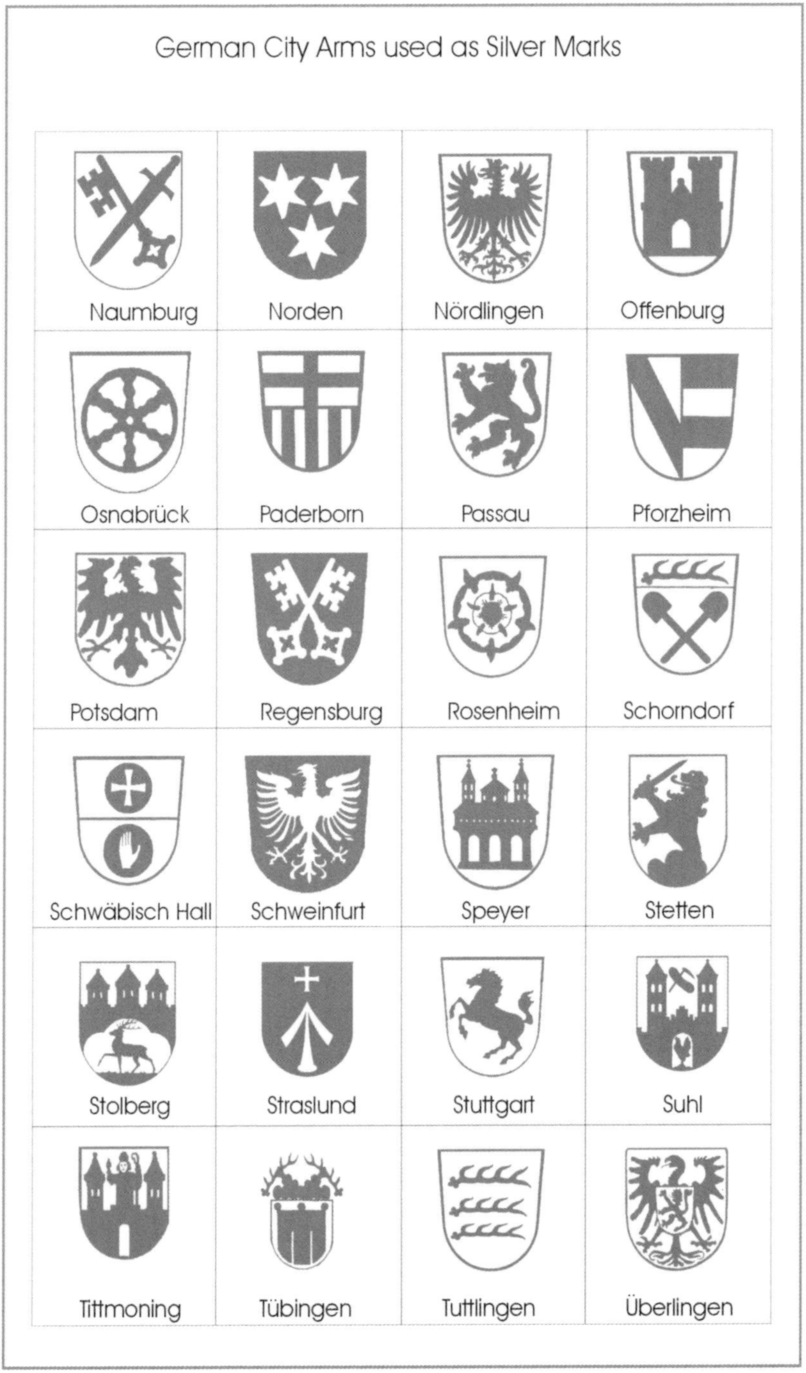

German City Arms used as Silver Marks

Naumburg	Norden	Nördlingen	Offenburg
Osnabrück	Paderborn	Passau	Pforzheim
Potsdam	Regensburg	Rosenheim	Schorndorf
Schwäbisch Hall	Schweinfurt	Speyer	Stetten
Stolberg	Straslund	Stuttgart	Suhl
Tittmoning	Tübingen	Tuttlingen	Überlingen

Figure 7-36: German City Arms used as Silver Marks, U to W

Figure 7-37: German hallmarks with a crown and crescent moon, .800 fineness

Great Britain – *see United Kingdom*

Holland – *see The Netherlands*

Hungary

1866 to 1937 – Austro-Hungarian silver was marked with four standards, .950 fineness, .900 fineness, .800 fineness, and .750 fineness. (See Austro-Hungarian history on page 103.)

In a decree in 1937, the Hungarian Government reduced the fineness of the first standard from .950 to .935. The fourth standard, .750, was dropped. The figures remained the same, but the shape of the shields changed.

Finally, the *Hungarian Official Gazette* published new standards on August 3, 1965.

Figure 7-38: Hungarian silver marks, 1867 to current

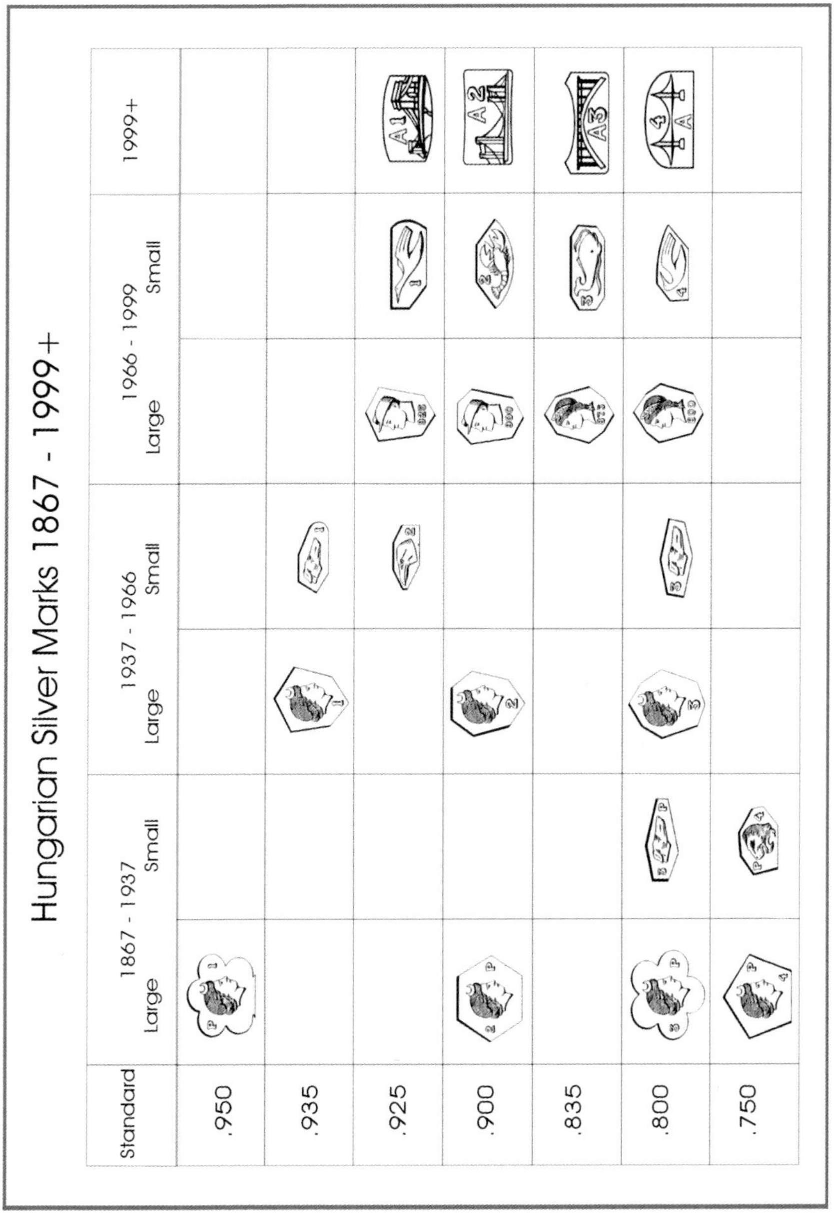

Ireland – *see United Kingdom*

Italy

1815 to 1872 – Italy was a country of individual kingdoms and states until it was unified in 1872. During this period, silver standards varied depending on who was in control of the region. Marks on Italian silver were influenced by reigning monarchs from the Austrian Empire, France, and Spain; the Vatican; and the Italians themselves.

The map in Figure 7-39 shows the political divisions as set by the Vienna Congress in 1815. Along with the regional divisions, the city of Naples remained a separate kingdom of the Bourbons.

Figure 7-39: Italy in 1815

There were different laws and different silver standards for every state. With the exception of Tuscany, the minimum standard for silverware was .800 fineness. The fineness standards are summarized below.

Lombardo-Venetian Kingdom before 1866 - .9375 and .750 fineness. **After 1866** - .950 fineness, .900 fineness, .800 fineness, and .750 fineness.

Parma - .917 and .792 fineness.

Sardinia and Piedmont - .950 and .800 fineness.

The Papal States - .937 and .875 fineness.

Tuscany - .987, .792, and .687 fineness.

Naples - .9155 and .8475 fineness.

What is most important about these divisions is that it can help us understand the types of marks we will see on Italian silver during this period.

If the silver is from the regions of Venezia, Lombardy, Parma, Modena, Lucca, and Tuscany, you should expect to see marks similar to those used in the Austrian Empire. This would be either an eagle (double or single head) with spread wings or marks similar to early 19th century Austrian marks. (See Figure 7-2.)

If the silver is from the regions of Piedmont and Sardinia, you will see marks with the coat of arms of the Italian House of Savoy, a crown above a shield with a Greek cross inside (Figure 7-40).

The city of Nice in France belonged to the Dukes of Savoy from 1388 until 1792. You will also see the Savoy coats of arms for silver produced in Nice in the late 18th century.

In the Papal states, which include the city of Rome, 17th and 18th century marks resemble the coat of arms of the Vatican, crossed keys with either a staff, cross or crown at the center. The keys symbolize the keys to the Kingdom of Heaven (Figure 7-41).

The city of Naples has a multi-national background. At various times in history, it has belonged to Spain, Northern Italy, Austria, France, and southern Italy. The most common marks found are the letters

Figure 7-40: First unified flag of Italy, 1863, with the arms of the House of Savoy

Figure 7-41: Vatican coat of arms, Palace of the Popes, France

"NAP," either alone or in combination with some other device.

Spain occupied the city of Naples, most recently in 1735. Many Spanish hallmarks use the same method and use the first three letters of the city name. While there is no documentation to support this influence, it is logical to make the connection.

The Papal States used *Bajocchi* to designate fineness in the early to mid 17th century. Bajocchi were represented with two digits. 95 Bajocchi = .844 fineness.

1873 to 1934 – In 1873 a law took effect permitting gold and silversmiths to work in any standard. Items could be submitted to the testing office which tested for three standards of silver: .950, .900, and .800 fineness. A uniform set of marks was put in place for the entire country. (See Figure 7-42.)

Most Italian silversmiths did not submit their pieces for assay, so these marks are rare on Italian silver. Most often, a simple number designation was used, such as 800 (with or without an outline), in addition to the maker's mark.

Italian Silver Marks 1873 - 1934

| 1st Standard .950 fineness | 2nd Standard .900 fineness | 3rd Standard .800 fineness |

Figure 7-42: Italian silver marks, 1873 to 1934

1935 to 1968 – A new law introduced in 1934 created uniform marking for silver. Silversmiths were assigned a number and a city code that appeared inside of a six-sided lozenge. A "fascio" was put in the center. The purity or fineness was shown in a separate mark inside an oval.

Figure 7-43: Italian lozenge with a "fascio"

Figure 7-44: Italian purity symbol for .800 fineness

In 1944, a law was passed to remove the fascio, as it was a symbol of fascism.

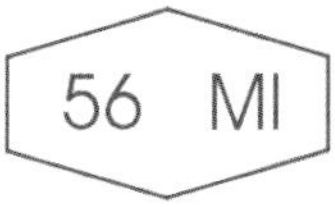

Figure 7-45: Italian lozenge without a "fascio"

1968 to present – The purity standards for assay were changed to .925, .835, and .800 fineness. New marks were struck to show the changes. The lozenge shaped changed, and a star was added to the inside before the maker's number and city code. This mark is required on all items except those intended for export. The purity symbol stayed the same, but with new assay standards.

Japan

The inaugural ceremony for the Japanese mint was held on April 4, 1871. Originally, the mint was established by the Meiji government to modernize the Japanese coinage system.

In 1929, the mint expanded to include the analysis and testing of metal ores and minerals, including the fineness certification of precious metal wares and hallmarking.

On May 18, 1954, Japanese Ministerial Ordinance Number 34 stated, in part: ". . . the hallmark will be issued for the valuable article and its chain on the request of the maker or dealer." The hallmark consists of a symbol, which is struck on the precious metal by the mint.

Article 16 of this order prescribed the symbols to be used. The prescribed symbols are the mark of the mint and the fineness mark. Additionally, silverware must also have the maker's mark. These are usually represented with Japanese characters.

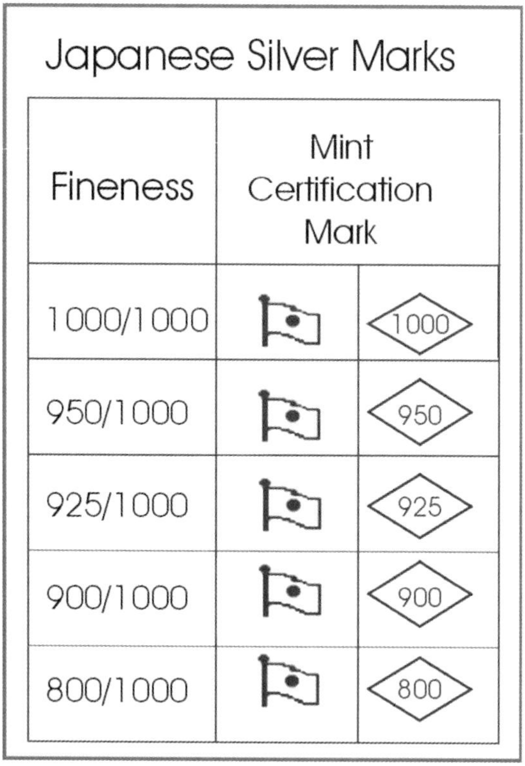

Japanese Silver Marks		
Fineness	Mint Certification Mark	
1000/1000		1000
950/1000		950
925/1000		925
900/1000		900
800/1000		800

Figure 7-47: Japanese maker's marks, assay marks and fineness marks.

Mexico

After World War II, the Mexican Government issued a guarantee mark in the shape of an eagle with spread wings and a snake in its mouth. Although originally the number in the middle was assigned to the city of assay, it was later modified to included maker's registered numbers. The system was abandoned in 1979, along with the eagle mark. At this time, the Mexican government instituted a series of registry numbers and letters that were registered to individual makers and workshops.

Figure 7-48: Mexico .925 fineness mark of the Union Nacional de Industriales de la Plata.

The Netherlands

1100 to 1795 – The Dutch established wealthy merchant towns during the 12th, 13th, and 14th centuries. Artisans and tradesmen were attracted to the cities for protection and patronage. 17th and 18th century marks reflect the coats of arms of various prosperous Dutch cities. Most coats of arms were combinations of a crown and shield flanked by a lion standing on its hind legs (a "rampant lion"), as shown in Figure 7-49.

Figure 7-49: Rotterdam Coat of Arms, image courtesy of the Bank Nederlandse Gemeenten

Silversmiths employed simplified versions using a shield with patterns and characters that symbolized their city, usually topped with a crown. A crown and shield with a rampant lion in the center represented the guaranteed fineness of .875. This fineness standard was in use until 1798.

Figure 7-50 shows silver marks in use during the 17th and 18th centuries that were based on local coats of arms. Compare the silver mark for Rotterdam to the coat of arms for Rotterdam.

The city of Amsterdam began using a system of date letters in 1503. Other towns adopted date-letter systems in the 16th, 17th, and 18th centuries. For most of these cities, letters of the alphabet were used consecutively from "A" to "X" or "Z," usually omitting the letters "J," "U" and "W."

Makers' marks varied but were usually initials in a shield with a device.

Silver Marking Under French Occupation

1795 to 1814 – In 1795, Napoleon conquered territories in Belgium, Luxembourg, and the Netherlands and called it the Batavian Empire. In November 1797, France introduced a new system for silver marking. The new system created departments, with cities in these departments being responsible for the assay of gold and silver, as shown in Figure 7-23.

All silver carried three marks: The fineness guarantee mark, the assay mark, and the maker's mark.

In 1798, the same system was set up for the Batavian Empire. Silver marks in the Netherlands from 1798 to 1809 and from 1809 to 1814 may look like French hallmarks. Makers were required to have their wares assayed and marked with one of two standards, .950 and .800 fineness, using the same rooster mark as that of French provinces (departments). Figure 7-51 shows the fineness marks used from 1798 forward.

Each assay department was assigned a number. The department number was included as part of the assay mark. Individual assay offices were set up within each department. Where there were two cities in the same department, a dot was placed after the letter. A third city in the department would receive two dots. (Figure 7-52).

Silver Marking in the Batavian Empire

In 1807, Napoleon Bonaparte transformed the Batavian Empire into the Kingdom of Holland. He made his third brother, Louis Napoleon, king of Holland.

The new king was anxious to gain the favor of the people in his new kingdom. One of the changes that he made was to create a new system for silver assay and hallmarking.

Louis Napoleon changed the standards from .950 and .800 fineness to .934 and .833 fineness. He created new marks for the fineness guarantee, the assay mark and the maker's mark. He also added date letters.

A crown in a hexagon was used as the guarantee mark for large items assayed at .934 fineness (Figure 7-51). The second standard of .800 fineness was marked with the number "10" in a rectangle, showing the amount of tax paid. Small items were marked with either the number "1" for the first standard or the number "2" for the second standard, each showing the amount of tax paid.

The assay marks were not new. Louis Napoleon took the city arms used by the Dutch guilds in the 17th and 18th centuries and simplified them into ovals. The size of the oval varied with the size of the item. Figure 7-53 is a partial list of assay marks used in the Kingdom of Holland.

The first date letter was added in October of 1808. The new system started with the letter "a" in lowercase script, as shown in Figure 7-54.

Silver Marking under French Annexation

In 1811, Napoleon conquered additional territories. At this time, the numbering system for the departments was modified and new departments were added (Figure 7-52).

Napoleon Bonaparte was not pleased with the changes his brother had made. In 1812 Napoleon annexed the Netherlands back to France, abolished the silver marking system his brother had established, and reinstated the French system with the new numbers for the departments. (See Figure 7-52.)

Silver Marking in the Netherlands

1814 to 1953 – With Napoleon defeated, the independence of The Netherlands was restored. New silver marks were created, and the standards set under the Kingdom of Holland, .934 and .833 fineness, were reinstated.

The first standard-guarantee mark for large items was a rampant lion with the number "1" under its paw, both enclosed in a shield. The second standard-guarantee mark was lion passant – that is, a lion walking with its head forward and its forepaw farther from the viewer raised – with the number "2" under its paw, both enclosed in a polygon. (See Figure 7-51.)

Second-standard small items were marked with a sword.

The assay stamp was the left-facing profile of a man wearing a cap. Each city of assay was assigned a letter. The letter is shown in the man's cap.

In 1814, the date letter was brought back, starting with the letter "E" in uppercase script. Notice that there is no date letter covering the period between February 1812 and 1813.

1953 to 1987 – In 1953, the Netherlands changed its silver standards to .925 and .835 fineness. A lion rampant continued to be used for the first standard, but the shape of the shield was changed and the Arabic number "1" was changed to the Roman numeral "I." The stamp for the second standard remained the same, but with the same substitution from an Arabic number "2" to a Roman numeral "II."

A dagger-shaped stamp with the fineness of either ".925" or ".835" was used for small items.

A third standard of .800 was introduced for watches. It was the letter "Z" and "800" enclosed in a polygon.

In 1953, a series of import marks were introduced for silver. The first standard of .925 fineness was represented by the letter "Z" and the Roman numeral "I" in a barrel-shaped lozenge. The second standard of .835 fineness was represented by the letter "Z" and the Roman numeral "II" in a barrel-shaped lozenge. The third standard of .800 fineness was represented by the letter "Z" alone, enclosed in a barrel-shaped lozenge.

At the same time, export marks were put into use. The maker was entitled to a tax refund if the item was exported out of the country. A key-shaped mark near the assay mark showed that the item was intended for export and eligible for the tax refund. These are often seen in Dutch territories.

1987 to present – In 1987, the .800 standard for watches was expanded to other items. It is represented by a reclining lion and the Roman numeral "III," both enclosed in a square.

Figures 7-50 through 7-54 show the changes in the Netherlands system of marking from 1798 to the present time.

Figure 7-50: Netherlands city arms used as silver marks (17th and 18th centuries)

Netherlands Fineness Standards with Marks in use from 1798 to Present

Distinction	1798 -1809	1807 - 1812		1809 -1814	1814 -1953		
		Large	Small		Large	Small	
1st Standard	 .950	 .934	 .934	 .950	 .934		
2nd Standard	 .800	 .833	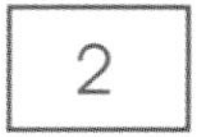 .833	 .800	 .833	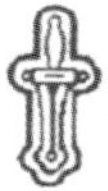 .833	 to1905 1906+

Distinction	1953 +		1987 +
	Large	Small	Large
1st Standard	 .925	 .925	
2nd Standard	 .835	 .835	.800
3rd Standard	.800 Watches		

From 1798 until 1814 the Netherlands was occupied by France. For a brief period between 1807 and 1812 Louis Napoleon ruled the Kingdom of Holland.

Displeased with his brother's pro-Dutch policies, Napoleon Bonaparte annexed the new Kingdom of Holland back to France and re-instated the former French marking system. The French system remained in effect, until he was defeated in 1814.

Figure 7-51: Netherlands standards, 1798 to present

144

Netherlands Assay Marks 1798 - to Present

	1798 -1809	1807 - 1812	1809 -1814	1814 -1905	1906+
Large Assay		Kingdom of Holland: Assay marks were based on city arms. See separate table of department assay marks.			
Medium Assay					
Small Assay				 (If possible)	 (If possible)

Netherlands Department Numbers 1798 - 1814

1798 - 1809	1809 - 1814		
Number	Number	Department	City
26	27	Dyle	Brussel
26•	27•	Dyle	Leuven
27	28	Escaut	Gent
27•	28•	Escaut	Gent
31	32	Forêts	Luxemburg
34	43	Jemmapes	Bergen
34•	43•	Jemmapes	Bergen
54	56	Lys	Brugge
54•	56•	Lys	Leper
62	65	Meuse-Infèrieur	Maastricht
62•	65•	Meuse-Infèrieur	Roemond
67	70	Duex-Nèthes	Antwerpen
	70•*	Duex-Nèthes	Breda
72	75	Ourthe	Luik
DR	86	Roer	Aken

*Opened in 1811

Figure 7-52: Netherlands assay marks, 1798 to present

145

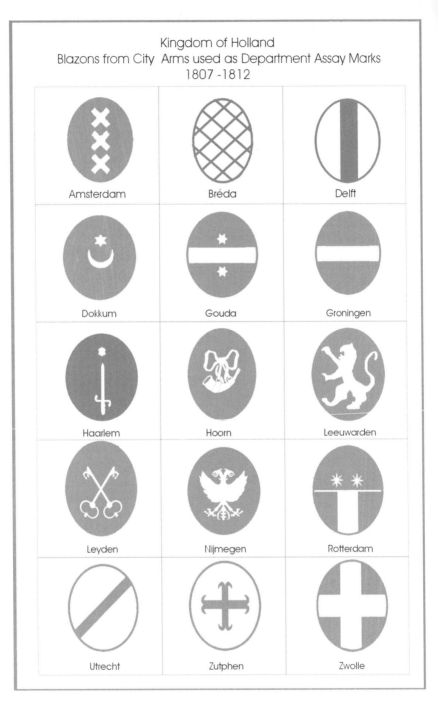

Figure 7-53: Kingdom of Holland assay marks, 1807 to 1812

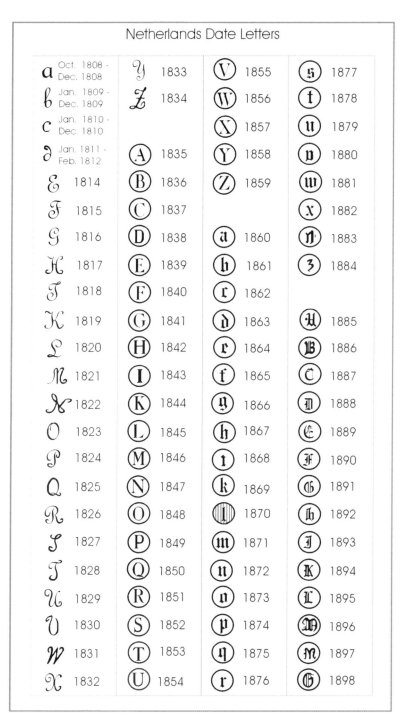

Netherlands Date Letters

a Oct. 1808 - Dec. 1808	𝒴 1833	Ⓥ 1855	ⓢ 1877
b Jan. 1809 - Dec. 1809	𝒵 1834	Ⓦ 1856	ⓣ 1878
c Jan. 1810 - Dec. 1810		Ⓧ 1857	ⓤ 1879
∂ Jan. 1811 - Feb. 1812	Ⓐ 1835	Ⓨ 1858	ⓥ 1880
ℰ 1814	Ⓑ 1836	Ⓩ 1859	ⓦ 1881
ℱ 1815	Ⓒ 1837		ⓧ 1882
𝒢 1816	Ⓓ 1838	ⓐ 1860	ⓨ 1883
ℋ 1817	Ⓔ 1839	ⓑ 1861	ⓩ 1884
ℐ 1818	Ⓕ 1840	ⓒ 1862	
𝒦 1819	Ⓖ 1841	ⓓ 1863	Ⓤ 1885
ℒ 1820	Ⓗ 1842	ⓔ 1864	Ⓑ 1886
ℳ 1821	Ⓘ 1843	ⓕ 1865	Ⓒ 1887
𝒩 1822	Ⓚ 1844	ⓖ 1866	Ⓓ 1888
𝒪 1823	Ⓛ 1845	ⓗ 1867	Ⓔ 1889
𝒫 1824	Ⓜ 1846	ⓘ 1868	Ⓕ 1890
𝒬 1825	Ⓝ 1847	ⓚ 1869	Ⓖ 1891
ℛ 1826	Ⓞ 1848	Ⓛ 1870	ⓗ 1892
𝒮 1827	Ⓟ 1849	ⓜ 1871	Ⓙ 1893
𝒯 1828	Ⓠ 1850	ⓝ 1872	Ⓚ 1894
𝒰 1829	Ⓡ 1851	ⓞ 1873	Ⓛ 1895
𝒱 1830	Ⓢ 1852	ⓟ 1874	Ⓜ 1896
𝒲 1831	Ⓣ 1853	ⓠ 1875	Ⓝ 1897
𝒳 1832	Ⓤ 1854	ⓡ 1876	Ⓖ 1898

Figure 7-54: Netherlands date letters, 1808 to 1898

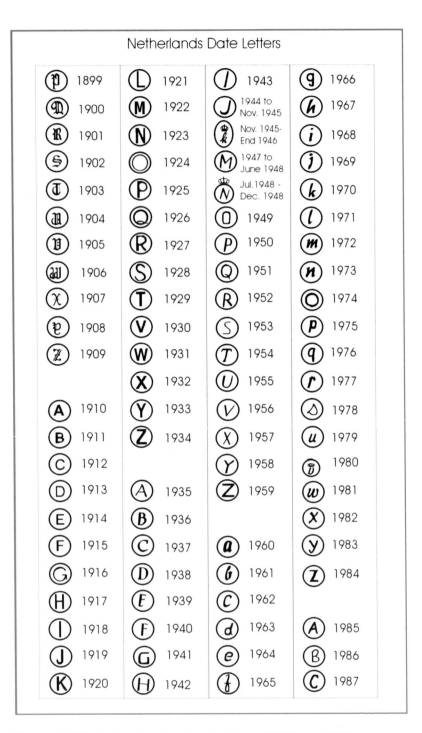

Netherlands Date Letters

℗	1899	Ⓛ	1921	Ⓘ	1943	ⓖ	1966
⑩	1900	Ⓜ	1922	Ⓙ	1944 to Nov. 1945	ⓗ	1967
ℝ	1901	Ⓝ	1923	Ⓚ	Nov. 1945-End 1946	ⓘ	1968
Ⓢ	1902	Ⓞ	1924	Ⓜ	1947 to June 1948	ⓙ	1969
Ⓣ	1903	Ⓟ	1925	Ⓝ	Jul.1948 - Dec. 1948	ⓚ	1970
ⓐ	1904	Ⓠ	1926	Ⓞ	1949	ⓛ	1971
ⓑ	1905	Ⓡ	1927	Ⓟ	1950	ⓜ	1972
ⓦ	1906	Ⓢ	1928	Ⓠ	1951	ⓝ	1973
Ⓧ	1907	Ⓣ	1929	Ⓡ	1952	Ⓞ	1974
ⓔ	1908	Ⓥ	1930	Ⓢ	1953	ⓟ	1975
ⓩ	1909	Ⓦ	1931	Ⓣ	1954	ⓠ	1976
		Ⓧ	1932	Ⓤ	1955	ⓡ	1977
Ⓐ	1910	Ⓨ	1933	Ⓥ	1956	ⓓ	1978
Ⓑ	1911	Ⓩ	1934	Ⓧ	1957	ⓤ	1979
Ⓒ	1912			Ⓨ	1958	ⓥ	1980
Ⓓ	1913	Ⓐ	1935	Ⓩ	1959	ⓦ	1981
Ⓔ	1914	Ⓑ	1936			Ⓧ	1982
Ⓕ	1915	Ⓒ	1937	ⓐ	1960	ⓨ	1983
Ⓖ	1916	Ⓓ	1938	ⓑ	1961	Ⓩ	1984
Ⓗ	1917	Ⓕ	1939	ⓒ	1962		
Ⓘ	1918	Ⓕ	1940	ⓓ	1963	Ⓐ	1985
Ⓙ	1919	Ⓖ	1941	ⓔ	1964	Ⓑ	1986
Ⓚ	1920	Ⓗ	1942	ⓕ	1965	Ⓒ	1987

Figure 7-55: Netherlands date letters, 1899 to 1987

Norway

1536 to 1814 – Norway was annexed to Denmark for nearly three hundred years. During that time, the silver trade that developed marked its wares with a system similar to the one used in Denmark, using the town mark for the fineness guarantee and a date mark. The fineness guarantee was a minimum of .830.

Assay offices were set up in Christiana (Oslo) in 1723, in Trondheim in 1723, and in Bergen in 1740. Bergen is probably the most significant center of silver manufacturing. The city of Stavanger was also an important center of silver production, although no assay office was ever established there.

Each city has an **assay mark**. The city of Bergen used a crowned letter "B" for its assay mark until 1740. After that, the city arms were used, a castle above seven dots. The castle was usually flanked by the year expressed in four digits. (See Figure 7-56.)

From 1781, the **date mark** was shown as a separate mark.

The **assayer's mark** was also required, usually shown by his initials.

Monthly marks were used beginning in 1740. Initially, they used numbers, but from 1766 to 1820 they used signs of the zodiac, and then returned the number system in 1821. (See Figures 7-58 and 7-59.) The fineness was shown in *lödig*, which is similar to the German löthige, with 16 löthige equal to pure silver:

> 16 lödig = 1.00 fineness (pure silver)
> 15 lödig = 0.9375 fineness
> 14 lödig = 0.875 fineness
> 13 lödig = 0.8125 fineness
> 12 lödig = 0.750 fineness

Expect to see figures like 12, 12-L, and 13½, for the **fineness mark**, sometimes (but not always) enclosed in a rectangle, as shown in Figure 7-60.

The **maker's mark** was either the silversmith's initials or the first letter of his name along with his last name.

From the late 18th century, expect to see five marks on silver from

Norway, although in many cases silver marking was not regulated closely and earlier silver often shows only the maker's mark.

1814 to 1891 – Norway was ceded to Sweden in 1814. Denmark had sided with Napoleon, who was defeated in 1814. Losing Norway to Sweden was part of the settlement. The Norwegians declared independence in 1814 but were invaded by Sweden. Agreement was reached whereby Norway remained an independent kingdom. They continued to use the same marking system, but it was not strictly enforced.

A law passed in 1884 allowed trademarks to be substituted for the maker's mark.

1891 to 1905 – Regulations that took effect in 1892 required that the fineness be marked in thousands. The minimum fineness was .830. Silver had to be marked 830S along with the maker's mark, usually his last name and first initial of his first name. Many export items and enameled items were worked as high as .925 fineness.

At this time, an official mark was added, a rampant lion enclosed in a circle, the national arms of Norway.

Assaying was not required, but if the silver was assayed by the Registered Assayer, his mark had to be added to the silver.

1905 to present – From about 1920, manufacturers began to use .925 fineness for domestic silver wares.

Figure 7-56: Bergen, Norway, silver mark, 1759

Figure 7-57: 1806 Bergen assay mark

Figure 7-58: 1806 year mark and zodiac sign

150

Zodiac Signs Used as Month Signs in Norway and Denmark

Capricorn	Aquarius	Pieces
♑	♒	♓
21/12 - 21/1	21/1 - 18/2	18/2 - 20/3
Dec. 21 - Jan. 21	Jan. 21 - Feb. 18	Feb. 18 - Mar. 20
Aries	Taurus	Gemini
♈	♉	II
20/3 - 20/4	20/4 - 21/5	22/5 - 21/6
Mar. 20 - Apr. 20	Apr. 20 - May 21	May 22 - Jun. 21
Cancer	Leo	Virgo
♋	♌	♍
21/6 - 22/7	22/7 - 21/8	21/8 - 23/9
Jun. 21 - Jul. 22	Jul. 22 - Aug. 21	Aug. 21 - Sep. 23
Libra	Scorpio	Sagittarius
♎	♏	♐
23/9 - 23/10	23/10 - 22/11	22/11 - 21/12
Sep. 23 - Oct. 23	Oct. 23 - Nov. 22	Nov. 22 - Dec. 21

Figure 7-59: Zodiac signs and numbering system used as monthly marks from 1740

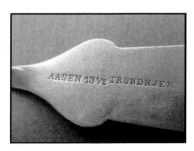

Figure 7-60: Norwegian fineness mark, 19th century

Figure 7-61: Norwegian assay mark of a crowned rampant lion, 1891 to 1905

151

Poland

Before 1772, Polish territory included Lithuania, Belarus, and half of Ukraine, which included the cities of Minsk in Belarus and Vilna in Lithuania. (See Figures 7-75 and 7-76 in Russia for Russian provinces.)

1772 to 1920 – In the late 18th century, due to wars with Prussia, Russia, and Austria, Poland was partitioned to the extent that it did not exist as a country and remained under foreign rule for most of the 19th century.

In the early 19th century, Poland sought help from Napoleon, who was defeated in 1814. The Congress of Vienna created the Kingdom of Poland, but it was only two-thirds its original size and remained under Russian control. The rest of Poland remained part of Prussia and Austria until after World War I.

The major cities for gold and silver making were Lemberg, Vilna, Krakow, and Warsaw.

Early marks reflected town or local guild marks, but silver marks during this period also reflected the marking system of the country that controlled that part of Poland.

Figure 7-62 shows a map of major cities in Poland. Those in the south were under Austrian control. The cities in the east were under Russian control. The cities in the north and west were under Prussian control.

Early 19th century marks in southern Poland resemble the same types of marks used by the Austrian Empire. (See Figure 7-2.) The number of löthige, usually 12 or 13, was at the top of the symbol, instead of the city letter. (See Germany or Austria Hungary for a list of fineness expressed in löthige.) For Krakow, a castle from the Krakow city coat of arms is shown in the center. A rampant lion is shown in the center for Lemberg. (See Figures 7-63 and 7-64.) Other southern Polish cities used the same method of marking.

The cities of Bochnia, Dukla, Jaroslaw, Jaslo, Lemberg, Premysl, Rzeszów, and Tarnów all used the Austrian system of silver marking until 1920.

Cities such as Gdansk (now Dantzig), Bydgoszcz, Poznan, and

Wroclaw were influenced by Prussia (Germany). Silver marking laws varied by region, and some areas had no formal laws at all.

Germany changed its silver marking laws in 1888. Before 1888, you would expect to see some portion of these cities' coats of arms as part of the silver mark. After 1888 you would see the German crescent moon and crown, along with the number "800," as shown in Figure 7-37.

Finally, the Russian marking system influenced the cities of Bialystok, Vilna, Warsaw, Lomza and Minsk. Russia opened assay offices in Lomza and Minsk in 1885.

The Russian system for marking is explained in detail under the section on Russian silver. As with other silver marks based on city coats of arms, you may find that only a portion of the arms was used for the silver mark. Poznan, for example, often used only the keys from the city arms.

1920 to present – Poland became a state after World War I.
Since the silver marking systems were influenced and controlled by other countries, the new Polish government ordered a census of all silver made and marked during the first world war. This silver was given a special census mark in addition to any other marks that were already on the piece.

If the silver was below .800 fineness but above .750 fineness, it received the "sword hilt" mark. These marks were used between 1920 and 1931.

Beginning in 1920, Poland had three standards for silver – .940 fineness, .875 fineness, and .800 fineness – most likely to accommodate the standards that different areas of Poland had been governed by for the previous 125 years. The standards and marks were changed in 1963 and again in 1986. These changes are shown in Figure 7-68.

There are currently ten assay offices in Poland. A single letter is used to represent each office.

A – Bialystok	L – Lódz
B – Bydgoszcz	P – Poznan
G – Gdansk	V – Wrochaw
H – Chorzów	W – Warsaw
K – Krakow	Z – Czestochowa

Figure 7-62: Map of Poland

Figure 7-63: Austro-Hungarian hallmarks used in Krakow, late 18th and 19th century

Figure 7-64: Austro-Hungarian hallmarks used in Lemberg, late 18th and 19th century

Figure 7-65: (See opposite page) Polish city arms with countries that influenced silver marking, 1772 to 1920

Figure 7-66: Polish census mark, 1920 to 1931

Figure 7-67: Polish "sword hilt" fineness mark, 1920 to 1931

Polish City Arms used as Silver Marks with the Countries that influenced Silver Marking

Bialystok	Bochnia	Bydgoszcz
Russia	Austria	Prussia
Dukla	Gdansk	Jaroslaw
Austria	Prussia	Austria
Krakow	Lemberg	Lomza
Austria	Austria	Russia
Minsk	Poznan	Przemysl
Russia	Prussia	Austria
Rzeszów	Stanislawow	Tarnow
Austria	Russia	Austria
Vilna	Warszawa	Wroclaw
Russia	Russia	Prussia

Figure 7-65: Polish city arms with countries that influenced silver marking, 1772 to 1920

155

Figure 7-68: Polish silver standards, 1920 forward

Standard	1920	1963	1986
.940	 1 W		
.925			 W 925
.916		 W 1	
.875	 2 W	 W 2	 K 875
.830			 P 830
.800	 3 W	 W 3	 G 800
.750		 W 4	

Portugal

1700 to 1800 – Silver was not mined in Portugal and had to be imported either in its unfinished state or as finished wares from Spain and Great Britain. As a result, silver from this period resembles that of Spain and Great Britain. Portuguese taste favored the English styles, and local silversmiths were known to forge English-type hallmarks on Portuguese wares.

During the reign of King John V, 1706 to 1750, silver became even scarcer. King John V acquired a tremendous amount of debt, and most of the local silver was melted down to pay the royal debts. In 1755 an earthquake and fire contributed to the loss of almost all of the remaining historically important silver.

Marks during this time were usually the first letter of the city, enclosed in a shield or cartouche and topped with a crown. The fineness standard was .958.

Lisbon (Lisboa) and Oporto have the longest history of silversmithing, with hallmarks traced back to the 15th century. There are also records of assay marks for Coimbra, Santarem, Beja, and Aveiro Giumares, Setubal, Evor, and Braga during this period as well.

1800 to 1886 – Portugal was engaged in several wars in the early part of the 19th century. A stable government did not emerge until the mid 19th century.

The practice of hallmarking with the first letter of the city of assay topped by a crown continued until 1886, when new marks were introduced. The city of Oporto used a crowned letter "P."

1882 to 1938 – At this time, there were four assay offices, Lisbon, Oporto, Gondomar, and Braga. The shield was a different shape for each city. Portugal had two standards for silver, .916 and .833 fineness, with separate marks for large and small items.

In **1882**, the boar and boar's head marks were introduced for tolerances of .005.

In **1886,** the tolerance was changed to .002. The new standard used an eagle for large items and an eagle's head for small items. The Roman numeral "I" was used for the first standard of .916 and "II" for the second standard of .833. The shape of the shield for Gondomar changed in 1913 for all standards.

After **1911**, silver was not assayed at Braga.

1938 to 1985 – In 1938, the symbols were changed. Instead of Roman numerals indicating the standard, the new marks had the fineness in thousandths imprinted under the eagle's chin, such as ("958" or ".958").

Small items used a rooster's head. The shield shapes remained the same.

1985 to present – Portugal changed its standards for silver fineness. Including ingots, there are five standards for silver: .999 fineness, .925 fineness, .835 fineness, .830 fineness, and .800 fineness. The head of an eagle is currently used to denote the various silver standards. The eagle's head faces left for the first two standards and right for the next three. The shapes of the shields remain the same.

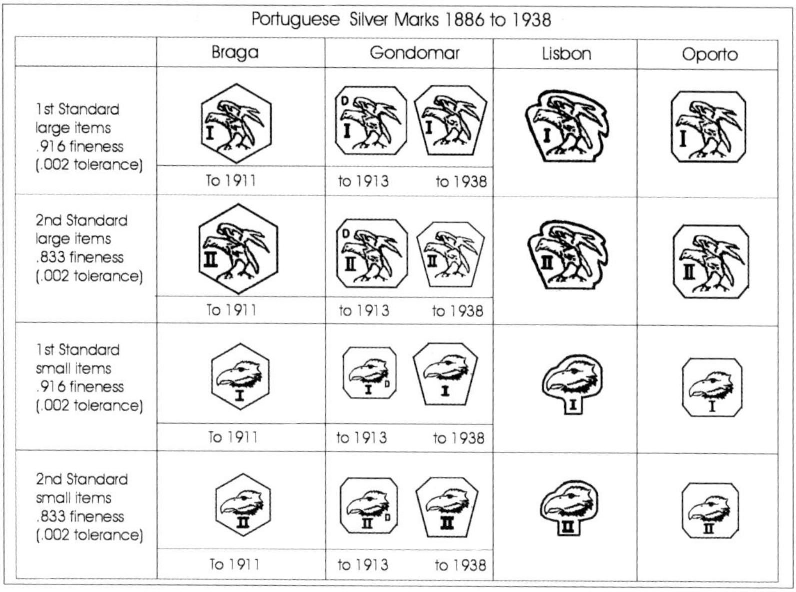

Portuguese Silver Marks 1886 to 1938

	Braga	Gondomar		Lisbon	Oporto
1st Standard large items .916 fineness (.002 tolerance)	To 1911	to 1913	to 1938		
2nd Standard large items .833 fineness (.002 tolerance)	To 1911	to 1913	to 1938		
1st Standard small items .916 fineness (.002 tolerance)	To 1911	to 1913	to 1938		
2nd Standard small items .833 fineness (.002 tolerance)	To 1911	to 1913	to 1938		

Figure 7-69a: Portuguese silver marks, 1882 to 1938

Figure 7-69b: Portuguese silver marks, .005+ tolerance, 1882 - 1938

1882 - 1938: .005 tolerance, only

The boar mark was used for large items with a greater tolerance of .005.

The boar's head mark was used for small items with a larger tolerance of .005.

The shield surrounding both the boar and the boar's head were the same shapes as the ones in use for each individual assay office.

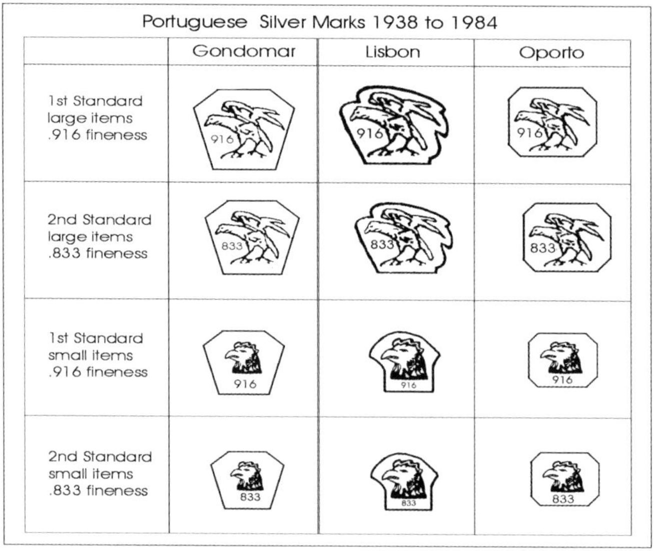

Portuguese Silver Marks 1938 to 1984

	Gondomar	Lisbon	Oporto
1st Standard large items .916 fineness	916	916	916
2nd Standard large items .833 fineness	833	833	833
1st Standard small items .916 fineness	916	916	916
2nd Standard small items .833 fineness	833	833	833

Figure 7-70: Portuguese silver marks, 1938 to 1984

Figure 7-71: Portuguese silver marks , 1985 to present

Portuguese Silver Marks 1985 to current

	Gondomar	Lisbon	Oporto
1st Standard .999 fineness (for ingots)	999	999	999
2nd Standard .925 fineness	925	925	925
3rd Standard .835 fineness	835	835	835
4th Standard .830 fineness	830	830	830
5th Standard .800 fineness	800	800	800

Russia

Silver Marking: 1613 to 1896

1613 to 1896 – There should be at least four marks on Russian silver before 1700, and five marks until 1896. (Figure 7-72).

Fineness Marking

Peter the Great introduced fineness marking in 1700. Although many standards were used, the most common were .875, .916, and .947. Russian silver was measured in *zolotniks* until 1925. Pure silver contained 96 zolotniks. Russian silver, then, is marked with the number of zolotniks, a two-digit number. This number will either be in one box or in one box for each digit.

Eighty-four zolotniks is actually .875 fineness.

$$84/96 = .875 \text{ fineness}$$
$$88/96 = .916 \text{ fineness}$$
$$91/96 = .947 \text{ fineness}$$

In practice, it appears that silver was marked with the actual silver content, so you may find old Russian silver marked "62," "72," or "94." If a silver item has a two-digit number, it is probably Russian or at least influenced by Russia at some time in the history of the country.

Assay Marks

Introduced and required in 1700, assay marks consisted of the initials of the assayer, enclosed in a rectangle and usually accompanied by the date. Sometimes they appeared with a scale. Assay marks in this form were used until 1896, when the entire marking system was simplified.

Maker's Marks

Maker's marks were also required beginning in 1700. There was no formal requirement for the mark; it could be the maker's initials in two or three letters, or it could be his entire last name, as Fabergé preferred. It could be enclosed in a rectangle, heart, or other shape and could include a device such as a flower or a bird. Maker's marks are often confused with assayer's marks.

Date Marks

For Moscow, date marks first appeared on either side of the eagle. In 1729, a separate mark was used for the date mark. It appeared beside or below the eagle until about 1735, when the date mark began to appear below the assayer's mark. Other cities followed.

City Marks

As we saw with The Netherlands, the origin for Russian silver marks is tied to the coats of arms of the various cities. Most Russian cities have origins several hundred years before the silver marking laws were established, and coats of arms were already in use as a means of identification. Usually only a portion of the heraldic device was used for silver, probably because silver marks are small. Using the entire device would have made it difficult to identify. For example, the city arms for Dorpat, in Estonia, is represented by two crossed keys over a castle. Most of the 17th and 18th century silver marks used only the crossed keys. Sometimes the keys were shown with a portion of the castle on either side of the keys. Riga had similar arms. The keys usually had a crown or a cross above them.

Figures 7-73 through 7-76 show the types of devices you would expect to see as Russian city marks on silver. The cities in Russia are shown first. The cities in the Russian Empire that are now independent countries are shown separately.

Moscow marks (1613 to 1896).
1613 to 1740 – Russian laws required Moscow silver to be marked since 1613. The mark was the imperial eagle, an eagle with two heads, enclosed in various-shaped shields.

1684 to 1700 – Moscow marks changed. A fineness mark with a date mark inside a circle replaced the eagle mark. The mark used Slavonic (Cyrillic) letters.

1700 – The two-headed eagle mark returned, using the date near the eagle in Slavonic letters.

1700 to 1710 – The two-headed eagle carries an orb and scepter in its talons.

1707 – The duties of the Russian mint and assay offices were combined. From this period forward, the eagle mark changed with changes in the coinage.

1733 to 1741 – The word "Mockba" (Moscow) appears under the eagle.

1741 – A mark showing Saint George and the dragon replaces imperial eagle mark. It is used until 1896.

Saint Petersburg marks (1700 – 1896).
1700 to 1735 – Silver made in Saint Petersburg was assayed in Moscow and marked with the imperial eagle. The letters "c n 6 " appeared underneath the eagle to distinguish between the two cities.

1735 to 1896 – On March 3, 1735, the city of Saint Petersburg was approved for silver testing. The mark consists of a scepter crossed by two anchors.

Marks of other Russian cities (1700 to 1896).

1700 – Peter the Great ordered that silver was to be marked in the Russian provinces. Originally, only Moscow silver items had marking requirements.

1773 – Russia began the process of training assay wardens for additional cities in Russia. Many of the assay offices were not established until the 19th century. By 1840, there were 43 assay offices in Russia. By 1863, there were 53.

Following are known dates of assay office openings and closings in various Russian cities.

1811 – Riga office opens

1825 – Ekaterinburg, Kiev, Odessa, Saratov, and Semipalatinsk offices open.

1870s – **Many assay offices were closed.** A partial list includes: Kishinev, Novgorod, Orel, Perm, Tobolsk, Tver, and Vologda.

1885 – Baku in Azerbaijan, Irkutsk in Siberia, Lomza in Poland, Minsk (Mazowiecki) in Poland, Tbilisi in Georgia, and Tobolsk in Siberia opened for assay.

Figure 7-72: Russian maker's mark, assayer's initials with date mark, fineness mark and city mark for Moscow

Silver Marking: 1896 to 1927

A law (*ukase*) passed in 1882 and took effect in 1896. This new law set four standards for fineness, still expressed in zolotniks: 84 (.875 fineness), 88 (.916 fineness), 91 (.947 fineness), and 95 (.989 fineness).

The city mark and the fineness mark were combined into one symbol. The city mark was placed next to the fineness number (expressed in zolotniks), usually enclosed in an oval, although some variations existed. (See Figure 7-77.)

Figure 7-73: Russian coats of arms used as silver hallmarks (A-0)

Russian Coats of Arms used as Silver Hallmarks
1613 to 1896

Astracha (Astrakhan)	Ekaterinburg	Galich (Galitz)	Irkutsk
Kaluga	Kazan	Kostroma	Kostroma
Kursk	Moscow	Moscow	Nizhny (Novgorod)
Nizhny (Novgorod)	Novocherkask	Orel	Orenburg

Figure 7-74: Russian coats of arms used as silver hallmarks (P–V)

Russian Coats of Arms used as Silver Hallmarks
1613 - 1896

Penza (Pénéa)	Pskov	Rostov	Ryazan (Rianzana)
Saratov	Semipalatinsk	Smolensk	St. Petersburg*
Tobolsk (tobolik)	Toropetz (Toropech)	Tula (Toula)	Tver (Tver Kalinin)
Ufa (Oufa)	Uglich (Ouglich)	Veliky Ustyug	Vladimir

*Also Petrograd, Leningrad

Figure 7-75: Coats of arms in Russian cities (V–Y) and Russian provinces used as silver hallmarks

Russian Coats of Arms used as Silver Hallmarks 1613 to 1896

| Vologda | Vorange (Voronezh) | Vyatka (Kirov) | Vyborg |
| Yaroslav | | | |

Coats of Arms used as Silver Hallmarks in Russian Provinces 1700 to 1896

Belarus	Estonia	Estonia	Estonia
Minsk (Mazowiecki)	Dorpat (Tartu)	Narva	Parnu (Pernau)
Estonia	Georgia	Latvia	Latvia
Tallinn (Revel)	Walk (Valga)	Tblisi	Bauska

Figure 7-76: Coats of arms used as silver hallmarks in Russian Provinces

Coats of Arms used as Silver Hallmarks in Russian Provinces
1700 to 1896

Latvia	Latvia	Latvia	Poland
Jelgava (Mitau)	Kuldiga (Goldingen)	Riga	Lomza

Ukraine	Ukraine	Ukraine	Ukraine
Chernihiv (Chernigov)	Kamenetz (Podolsk)	Kharkiv (Kharkov)	Kiov (Kyiv, Kikev, Kiev)

Ukraine	Ukraine
Odesa	Zhytomyr

Date Marks

Date marks continued to be required. (See Figure 7-72.)

National Mark and District Mark

1896 – A national mark was introduced. It was the left-facing profile of a woman wearing a Kokosnik, which is a traditional Russian headdress worn by married women. It also showed the fineness in zolotniks. Each district had an assayer. The assayer's initials in Cyrillic letters were placed to the right of the profile.

1908 to 1917 – The national mark faced right, and the shape of the shield varied. Instead of the assayer's initials, a Greek number was used to represent each district.

Figure 7-77: Combined fineness and city mark, 1896 to 1927

Figure 7-78: Russian "Kokosnik" mark, 1896 to 1908

Figure 7-79: Russian "Kokosnik" mark, 1908 to 1917

Maker's Marks

The maker's marks consisted of the initials of the first and last name of the maker.

Silver Marking: 1927 to 1958

A new mark was introduced for the national mark. It was a right-facing workman's head with the district number shown in Cyrillic characters. The fineness was indicated in thousands, not zoloniks. The shape of the shield varied.

Figure 7-80: Russian worker's head marks

Silver Marking: 1958 to Present

In 1958, a new mark was introduced for the national mark: a hammer and sickle inside a five-pointed star. The fineness, in thousandths, appeared with the new mark. The district mark continues to be used. It is near the star.

Figure 7-81: Russian hammer and sickle mark

167

Scotland – *see United Kingdom*

Spain

Fineness

1497 to 1933 – In 1497, an ordinance of the Medina de Campo set the fineness for silver coin at .930. The consistency and purity of Spanish coin set the standards for the world for the next two hundred years.

The practice of measuring silver in *dineros* and *granos* was established under this ordinance.

> 12 dineros = pure silver
> 11 dineros = .916 fineness
> 9 dineros = .750 fineness
>
> 24 granos = 1 dinero

In 1626, sample coins were assayed in England and found to be between .925 and .916 fineness.

In 1642, King Philip IV of Spain instituted a tax on silver to help finance the thirty-year war to stop revolts in Catalonia (now part of Spain) and Portugal. The tax was called the "Quinto," or the King's fifth. It placed a 20% tax on silver and silver products imported into Spain. The "Quinto" discouraged the marking of silver in an attempt to avoid the tax.

In the same year, King Philip also passed a law permitting two standards of coin, one to be used in Spain and one to be used in the colonies. The fineness for the new coin was about .744. The domestic coin had about 20% less silver than the coins made for the colonies. This is the most probable date for the introduction of the two silver standards we see for Spanish silver items, .916 and .750 fineness.

1933 to present -The practice of measuring fineness in dineros continued until the marking laws changed in 1934, at which time, fineness was measured in thousandths, adjusting the first standard from .916 to .915.

In 2004, Spain changed the first standard to .925 and the second standard to .800 to comply with Hallmarking Convention Requirements. Ingots must have a fineness of .999.

Marks

1497 to 1933 –Other than for coinage, the assay and marking of silver was left up to the various guilds, with no formal laws for marking. In practice, coats of arms of the various towns were used as an assurance of fineness. As we have seen with other countries, part or all of the arms could be used as silver hallmarks. Figures 7-82, 7-83 and 7-84 represent a partial list of hallmarks compared to coats of arms.

Since there were no rules for marking silver, there is some overlap in the use of marks. Avila, Cacares, and Valencia all used crowns. Cordoba and Zaragoza both used a rampant lion. One solution may have been to spell out the name of the city or use a portion of the city's name along with the town arms. This may be one reason why many early Spanish marks used the city name, a partial city name, or initials such as "Avila," "Bar" (Barcelona), or "Burg" (Burgos).

Many Spanish towns used text or letters in their town arms. For example, the city of Valencia used the letters "LL" in their town arms. One story is that the city of Valencia was twice loyal to King Jaume I of Catalunya. *Leal* is Spanish for *loyal.*

If your mark has city names spelled out or initials, try to match it to a Spanish city first.

You may also find date marks. It was not a common practice, but some makers added date marks as far back as the 17th century, and the practice continued into the early 20th century. Usually only the last two digits of the year are represented.

In the late 19th century, we see some attempts to mark Spanish silver with the fineness in *dineros*, but it was not mandatory. Expect to see town marks with "9 D" or "11D," although other fineness marks are found.

1934 to 2004 – New laws went into effect setting standards of testing and standards of fineness. The fineness requirements changed slightly, with .915 for the first standard while the second remained at .750, which was permitted for small items only.

Assay offices were assigned a letter.

Baleares: PM
Barcelona: B
Cordoba: CO
Coruña: C
Granada: GR
Guipuzcoa: SS

Madrid: M
Salamanca: SA
Sevilla: SE
Valencia: V
Vizcaya: BI
Zaragoza: Z

All silver must have two marks. The first mark is for the fineness. A star inside an oval represents .915 fineness. A shooting star inside a square represents .750 fineness.

The second mark is the maker's mark and the city of assay inside a hexagram. The second mark may also be the importer's mark inside a triangle with the city of assay.

2004 to present – In addition to changing the standards to comply with Hallmarking Convention, requirements, Spain now assays silver at .999, .925, and .800 fineness with new marks for a new standards. The new mark combines the numeric fineness with the initial for the assay office inside a rectangle.

New assay offices have opened with new letters to represent each office.

Andalucia: A
Aragon: AR
Asturias: AS
Baleares: B
Canaria: CS
Castilla La Mancha: CM
Castilla Leon: CL
Cataluña: C

Extremadura: E
Galicia: G
La Rioja: R
Madrid: M
Murcia: MU
Navarra: N
Vizcay: PV
Valencia: V

The maker's mark or importer's mark is still required as shown in Figure 7-85.

Figure 7-82: Spanish city marks and hallmarks (B–G) 1497 to 1933

Spanish City Arms and Silver Hallmarks

Barcelona	Barcelona	Barcelona	Bilbao
Coat of Arms	Hallmark (17th c.)	Hallmark (17th c.)	Coat of Arms
Bilbao	Caceres*	Cadiz	Cadiz
Hallmark (17th c.)	Coat of Arms	Coat of Arms	Hallmark
Calatayud*	Cordoba	Cordoba	Estrella
Coat of Arms	Coat of Arms	Hallmark	Coat of Arms
Estrella	Gerona*	Granada	Granada
Hallmark	Coat of Arms	Coat of Arms	Hallmark

*Hallmark not available

Figure 7-83: Spanish city marks and hallmarks (J-H), 1497 to 1933

Spanish City Arms and Silver Hallmarks

Jaen*	Logrono	Logrono	Logrono
Coat of Arms	Coat of Arms	Hallmark (18th c.)	Hallmark (19th c.)
Lugo	Lugo	Madrid	Madrid
Coat of Arms	Hallmark	Coat of Arms	Hallmark
Madrid	Ronda	Ronda	San Sebastian
Hallmark 1805	Coat of Arms	Hallmark	Coat of Arms
San Sebastian	San Sebastian	Santiago de Compostela	Santiago de Compostela
Hallmark (16th c.)	Hallmark (16th c.)	Coat of Arms	Hallmark

*Hallmark not available

Figure 7-84: Spanish city marks and hallmarks (S–Z), 1497 to 1933

Figure 7-85: Spanish .915 fineness mark, maker's mark and importer's mark

Figure 7-86: Spanish .925 fineness mark combined with assay office, 2004 to present

Sweden

1485 – In 1485, the King of Sweden decreed that goldsmiths and silversmiths must put their mark on wares they made. The oldest known marks do not appear until about 100 years later. Expect to see two or more initials, or a monogram combined with a kind of trademark.

1596 – Goldsmiths and silversmiths were required to imprint their town's coat of arms, along with their maker's mark. A partial list has been provided in Figures 7-87, 7-88, and 7-89.

Just as with other guilds that used city arms as silver hallmarks, in some instances only a portion of the arms was chosen for the silver mark, especially if the arms had many different images. For the city of Landskrona, you usually see the cornucopia of the arms; Strängnäs used just the keys. Stockholm used just the crown from St. Erik's portrait. Stockholm is one of the oldest cities in Sweden to use city marks.

1689 – Date letters were required in addition to the city mark and maker's mark. Stockholm began using St. Erik's head, crowned as shown in figure 7-88. From 1715 to 1850, St. Erik's head is shown in profile.

1754 – A decree dated December 7, 1752, went into effect in 1754 and introduced the national mark. The national mark was the coat of arms for Sweden, three crowns in a trefoil. This mark guaranteed a fineness of .813 lods (see Finland), or .830 fineness. The letter "S" in a six-sided lozenge represents this fineness.

At the same time, date letters were standardized for the entire country. The date letter consisted of a letter of the alphabet, except "J" and "W." The letter "A" was used in 1759. A number was added in 1783. The serial number changed every twenty-four years. Both were enclosed in a rectangle. Thus, the date letter for 1759 was "A." The date letter for 1783 was "A2." If you add twenty-four years to 1783, you get 1807. The date letter for 1807 is "A3" (Figure 7-92).

1860 – Sometime around 1860, the city coat of arms was replaced. The first letter of the city was used inside a circle, square, triangle, or diamond. Different fonts were used for cities whose names began with the same letter. Stockholm began to use the head of St. Erik facing forward again and in a circle. These were used in addition to the state control mark and fineness mark. A sample list is shown in Figure 7-93.

Figure 7-87: Swedish city arms used as hallmarks (A–L)

175

Figure 7-88: Swedish city arms used as hallmarks (L–U)

Swedish City Arms used as Silver Hallmarks

Linköping	Luleå	Lund	Malmö
Norrköping	Nyköping	Orebro	Pitea
Sala	Söderhamn	Söderköping	Stockholm
Strängnäs	Sundsval	Uddevallea	Umea

Figure 7-89: Swedish city arms used as hallmarks (V–Y)

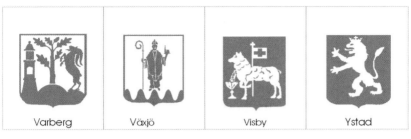

| Varberg | Växjö | Visby | Ystad |

Figure 7-90: Swedish national mark, introduced in 1754

Figure 7-91: Swedish fineness mark, introduced in 1754

1759 A	1783 A2	1807 A3	1831 A4	1855 A5
1760 B	1784 B2	1808 B3	1832 B4	1856 B5
1761 C	1785 C2	1809 C3	1833 C4	1857 C5
1762 D	1786 D2	1810 D3	1834 D4	1858 D5
1763 E	1787 E2	1811 E3	1835 E4	1859 E5
1764 F	1788 F2	1812 F3	1836 F4	1860 F5
1765 G	1789 G2	1813 G3	1837 G4	1861 G5
1766 H	1790 H2	1814 H3	1838 H4	1862 H5
1767 I	1791 I2	1815 I3	1839 I4	1863 I5
1768 K	1792 K2	1816 K3	1840 K4	1864 K5
1769 L	1793 L2	1817 L3	1841 L4	1865 L5
1770 M	1794 M2	1818 M3	1842 M4	1866 M5
1771 N	1795 N2	1819 N3	1843 N4	1867 N5
1772 O	1796 O2	1820 O3	1844 O4	1868 O5
1773 P	1797 P2	1821 P3	1845 P4	1869 P5
1774 Q	1798 Q2	1822 Q3	1846 Q4	1870 Q5
1775 R	1799 R2	1823 R3	1847 R4	1871 R5
1776 S	1800 S2	1824 S3	1848 S4	1872 S5
1777 T	1801 T2	1825 T3	1849 T4	1873 T5
1778 U	1802 U2	1826 U3	1850 U4	1874 U5
1779 V	1803 V2	1827 V3	1851 V4	1875 V5
1780 X	1804 X2	1828 X3	1852 X4	1876 X5
1781 Y	1805 Y2	1829 Y3	1853 Y4	1877 Y5
1782 Z	1806 Z2	1830 Z3	1854 Z4	1878 Z5

Figure 7-92: Swedish date letters, introduced in 1759

Figure 7-92 (continued): Swedish date letters, introduced in 1759

1879 **A 6**	1903 **A 7**	1927 **A 8**	1951 **A 9**
1880 **B 6**	1904 **B 7**	1928 **B 8**	1952 **B 9**
1881 **C 6**	1905 **C 7**	1929 **C 8**	1953 **C 9**
1882 **D 6**	1906 **D 7**	1930 **D 8**	1954 **D 9**
1883 **E 6**	1907 **E 7**	1931 **E 8**	1955 **E 9**
1884 **F 6**	1908 **F 7**	1932 **F 8**	1956 **F 9**
1885 **G 6**	1909 **G 7**	1933 **G 8**	1957 **G 9**
1886 **H 6**	1910 **H 7**	1934 **H 8**	1958 **H 9**
1887 **I 6**	1911 **I 7**	1935 **I 8**	1959 **I 9**
1888 **K 6**	1912 **K 7**	1936 **K 8**	1960 **K 9**
1889 **L 6**	1913 **L 7**	1937 **L 8**	1961 **L 9**
1890 **M 6**	1914 **M 7**	1938 **M 8**	1962 **M 9**
1891 **N 6**	1915 **N 7**	1939 **N 8**	1963 **N 9**
1892 **O 6**	1916 **O 7**	1940 **O 8**	1964 **O 9**
1893 **P 6**	1917 **P 7**	1941 **P 8**	1965 **P 9**
1894 **Q 6**	1918 **Q 7**	1942 **Q 8**	1966 **Q 9**
1895 **R 6**	1919 **R 7**	1943 **R 8**	1967 **R 9**
1896 **S 6**	1920 **S 7**	1944 **S 8**	1968 **S 9**
1897 **T 6**	1921 **T 7**	1945 **T 8**	1969 **T 9**
1898 **U 6**	1922 **U 7**	1946 **U 8**	1970 **U 9**
1899 **V 6**	1923 **V 7**	1947 **V 8**	1971 **V 9**
1900 **X 6**	1924 **X 7**	1948 **X 8**	1972 **X 9**
1901 **Y 6**	1925 **Y 7**	1949 **Y 8**	1973 **Y 9**
1902 **Z 6**	1926 **Z 7**	1950 **Z 8**	1974 **Z 9**

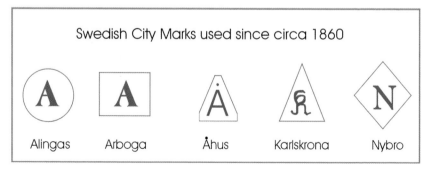

Swedish City Marks used since circa 1860

Alingas   Arboga   Åhus   Karlskrona   Nybro

Figure 7-93: Sample of Swedish city letters from c. 1860

Switzerland

1790 to 1815 – Switzerland is divided into cantons, small municipalities within the country. Hallmarking rules varied from canton to canton, but most cities used the arms of the city or the arms of the canton along with the maker's mark to hallmark silver. The arms for the various cantons do not have crowns or other external ornaments, so you will not generally see them on early Swiss silver.

Before 1800 the standards for silver fineness ranged from .750 to .916 fineness.

The city and canton of Geneva used three standards – .910, .833, and .750 fineness – each fineness receiving a different hallmark. The arms of Geneva were used for the first standard of .910. (See Figure 7-94.) The second standard of .833 required the maker's mark to be stamped twice. The third standard of .750 required the maker's mark to be stamped one time only.

With the help of Napoleon Bonaparte, Switzerland's cantons were unified as the Helvetic Republic in 1798. The French occupied Switzerland until 1803, at which time Napoleon granted a new constitution.

In 1815, the Congress of Vienna recognized the neutrality of Switzerland and expanded the country to include 22 cantons.

1815 to 1881 – The canton of Geneva appears to have been influenced by the occupation of the French, changing their silver standards and marks in 1815. The first standard was raised to .950 fineness, the standard required in France; the second and third standards remained the same. The first standard consisted of an eagle's head in profile with the number "1". The second standard was horse's head in profile with the number "2." The third standard was the full front face of a lion with the number "3." A crown was used as the guarantee mark for all three standards. All are shown in Figure 7-95.

Standards for the other cantons during this time are as follows:

Canton Basle required a minimum fineness of .7875.

Canton Glarus, from 1761, required a minimum fineness of .750.

Canton Lucerne, from 1804, required a minimum fineness of .800.

Canton Neufchatel first established silver standards in 1754, with a minimum fineness requirement of .800. The Neufchatel assay office was reorganized in 1852, at which time the chevron from the town arms was used to indicate a fineness of .800 (Figure 7-96).

Canton Pay de Vaud established silver regulations beginning in 1848, using two standards for silver, .900 fineness and .800. Regulations required that the name of the manufacturer and the fineness be marked on all silver.

Canton Zurich had three major centers of silver production, Zurich, Winterthur, and Elgg.

1880 to 1934 – In 1880, a Federal Act fixed standards for all Swiss silver. The allowable standards were .935, .925, .900, .875, and .800, probably in an attempt to accommodate the standards of various cantons. A transitional mark of a bee was stamped on all wares that met any of these standards.

From 1882 to 1934, Swiss-made silver had two standards, .875 fineness and .800 fineness. A rampant bear was used for the first standard of .875, and a grouse was used for the second standard of .800 fineness. Both marks had a letter or symbol for the assay office where the "x" is shown in Figure 7-97. The shapes of the shields were different for small articles.

Since July 1, 1934, all silverware must have the maker's mark. Hallmarking is required for watchcases. Assay is optional for exported silverware for other items.

1934 to Present - In 1995, a new hallmark was introduced, the Saint Bernard Dog head. It represents .925 fineness, and the assay is optional.

Figure 7-94: Swiss city arms

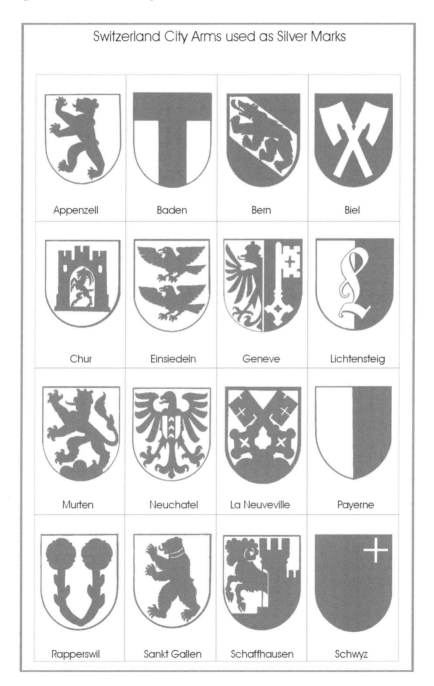

Switzerland City Arms used as Silver Marks

Appenzell	Baden	Bern	Biel
Chur	Einsiedeln	Geneve	Lichtensteig
Murten	Neuchatel	La Neuveville	Payerne
Rapperswil	Sankt Gallen	Schaffhausen	Schwyz

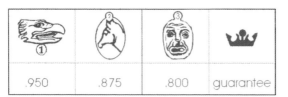

**Figure 7-95:
Geneva canton
silver marks, 1815
to 1881**

.950	.875	.800	guarantee

**Figure 7-96: 1852
Neufchatel hallmark for
.800 silver**

Swiss Hallmarks 1882 - 1934

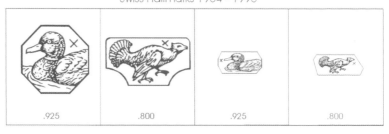

Large Items		Small Items	
.875+	.800	.875	.800

Swiss Hallmarks 1934 - 1995

.925	.800	.925	.800

Figure 7-97: Swiss marks used from 1882 to 1995

**Figure 7-98: Swiss St.
Bernard Dog head, .925
fineness**

United Kingdom

In 1238, King Henry III of England instituted the assay of gold and silver to prevent fraud. The law also prescribed that all items made of silver to be 925 parts silver to 75 parts copper, the same as the coin of the realm.

Over the next few hundred years, many laws were passed to control the quality of silver. The result is that we can trace English silver back to the year it was assayed by learning the basic marking system they used. A premium is placed on English silver because of the ability to date a piece by reading its hallmarks.

Expect to see at least four marks on a piece of English silver: The quality mark, the town mark, the maker's mark, and the date letter.

Quality Mark

1300 – The leopard's head was used to show the silver fineness of .925.

1336 – The crowned leopard's head was used to show the silver fineness.

1545 – The crowned lion passant (the lion, walking on all fours, head facing forward and one paw raised) is used to denote fineness.

1549 – The lion passant loses its crown.

Figure 7-99: Crowned lion passant

Figure 7-100: Lion passant

Town Mark

Originally, London was the only city where assaying of silver was allowed. In 1363, powers to assay were granted to the various towns.

Each city had its own mark. London used the crowned leopard's head. Edinburgh used a castle. Dublin used a harp. The other cities are shown, along with the complete hallmark system, at the end of the section (Figure 7-104).

Maker's Mark

The maker's mark was required as early as 1327 in some towns. Most people were illiterate, so the maker's mark was usually a symbol. By 1720, when illiteracy was no longer a widespread issue, silversmiths began using their initials to mark their wares.

Date Mark

The date mark consists of a letter inside a shield. The individual assay offices varied slightly in procedure, but basically, a new letter was used for each year, beginning with "A" until the end of the alphabet was reached.

London, for example, went in twenty-year cycles, excluded the letter J and stopping at "U" or "V." The font of the letters would change with each complete cycle, along with the shape of the shield. Sheffield went all the way to "Z" in the alphabet.

Other Marks on English Silver

The Duty Mark was used from 1784 to 1890. This is an easy way to date late 18th and 19th century silver as it covers roughly one hundred years. It is also called the sovereign's head and represented payment of a tax placed on silver. It looks like the reigning king or queen in profile. Small silver items were exempt from this tax. It is important to note that many small silver items were exempt from hallmarking altogether.

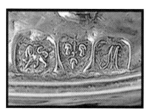

Figure 7-101: 1912 English hallmarks, Chester assay office, left to right: quality mark, town mark, and date

The British Import Mark was required on all imported silver and gold from 1867 to 1904 and is represented by the letter "F." From 1842 to 1904, imports had to be assayed in England before they could be sold. In 1904, imports

Figure 7- 102: London hallmarks with import mark

were marked with the decimal value of the standard used, such as .925.

Three **Commemorative Marks** were used in the twentieth century: the *Jubilee Mark* (1934-1935) the *Coronation Mark* (1952-1953) and the *Silver Jubilee Mark* (1977). Be careful, because at first glance they can look like duty marks.

There have been many assay offices in Britain's long history of hallmarking, but today there are only four in Great Britain: Birmingham, Edinburgh, London, and Sheffield. An easy way to remind yourself is to think of silver B.E.L.S.

Birmingham	Edinburgh	London	Sheffield
United Kingdom			

Figure 7-103: Town marks for current English assay offices

⚓ 🦁		🔵 Q 1788		🔵 f 1803		
A 1773		🔵 R 1789		🔵 g 1804		
A 1773		🔵 S 1790		🔵 h 1805		
A 1773		🔵 T 1791		🔵 i 1806		
B 1774		🔵 U 1792		🔵 j 1807		
C 1775		🔵 V 1793		🔵 k 1808		
D 1776		🔵 W 1794		🔵 l 1809		
E 1777		🔵 X 1795		🔵 m 1810		
F 1778		🔵 Y 1796		🔵 n 1811		
G 1779		🔵 Z 1797		🔵 o 1812		

For a short time in 1797, the king's head was stamped twice because the duty on silver was doubled.

⚓ 🦁

🔵 a 1798		🔵 p 1813
🔵 b 1799		🔵 q 1814
🔵 c 1800		🔵 r 1815
🔵 d 1801		🔵 s 1816
🔵 e 1802		🔵 t 1817

H 1780
I 1781
K 1782
L 1783
🔵 M 1784
🔵 N 1785
🔵 O 1786
🔵 P 1787

🔵 u 1818
🔵 v 1819
🔵 w 1820

Figure 7-104: English hallmarking system, Birmingham to York

🜋 𝕏 1821	😀 ℙ 1838	😀 G 1855
🜋 𝕪 1822	😀 ℚ 1839	😀 H 1856
🜋 ℤ 1823	😀 ℝ 1840	😀 I 1857
⚓ 🦁	😀 𝕊 1841	😀 J 1858
😀 𝔄 1824	😀 𝕋 1842	😀 K 1859
😀 𝔅 1825	😀 𝕌 1843	😀 L 1860
😀 ℭ 1826	😀 𝕍 1844	😀 M 1861
😀 𝔇 1827	😀 𝕎 1845	😀 N 1862
😀 𝔈 1828	😀 𝕏 1846	😀 O 1863
😀 𝔉 1829	😀 𝕐 1847	😀 P 1864
😀 𝔊 1830	😀 ℤ 1848	😀 Q 1865
😀 𝔥 1831	⚓ 🦁	😀 R 1866
😀 𝔍 1832	😀 A 1849	⚓ 🦁
😀 𝔎 1833	😀 B 1850	😀 S 1867
😀 𝔏 1834	😀 C 1851	😀 T 1868
😀 𝔐 1835	😀 D 1852	😀 U 1869
😀 𝔑 1836	😀 E 1853	😀 V 1870
😀 𝔒 1837	😀 F 1854	😀 W 1871

X	1872
Y	1873
Z	1874

a	1875
b	1876
c	1877
d	1878
e	1879
f	1880
g	1881
h	1882

i	1883
k	1884
l	1885
m	1886
n	1887

o	1888
p	1889
q	1890

After 1890 the duty mark was no longer used.

r	1891
s	1892
t	1893
u	1894
v	1895
w	1896
x	1897
y	1898
z	1899

a	1900
b	1901
c	1902
d	1903

e	1904
f	1905
g	1906
h	1907
i	1908
k	1909
l	1910
m	1911
n	1912
o	1913
p	1914
q	1915
r	1916
s	1917

t	1918
u	1919
v	1920

W 1921	M 1936	C 1952
X 1922	N 1937	D 1953
y 1923	O 1938	(anchor) (lion)
Z 1924	P 1939	E 1954
(anchor) (lion)	Q 1940	F 1955
A 1925	R 1941	G 1956
B 1926	S 1942	H 1957
C 1927	T 1943	J 1958
D 1928	U 1944	K 1959
E 1929	V 1945	L 1960
F 1930	W 1946	M 1961
G 1931	X 1947	N 1962
H 1932	Y 1948	O 1963
J 1933	Z 1949	P 1964
(anchor) (lion)	(anchor) (lion)	2 1965
K 1934	A 1950	(anchor) (lion)
L 1935	B 1951	R 1966
(anchor) (lion)	(anchor) (lion)	S 1967

189

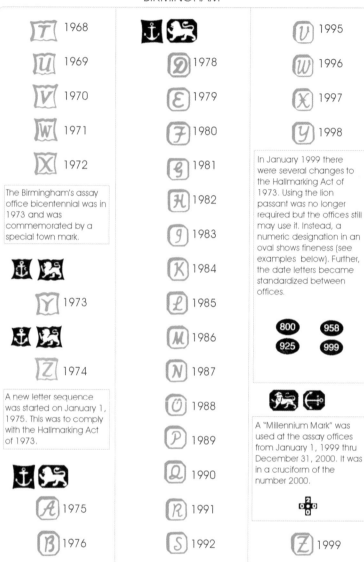

T 1968

U 1969

V 1970

W 1971

X 1972

The Birmingham's assay office bicentennial was in 1973 and was commemorated by a special town mark.

Y 1973

Z 1974

A new letter sequence was started on January 1, 1975. This was to comply with the Hallmarking Act of 1973.

A 1975

B 1976

C 1977

D 1978

E 1979

F 1980

G 1981

H 1982

I 1983

K 1984

L 1985

M 1986

N 1987

O 1988

P 1989

Q 1990

R 1991

S 1992

T 1993

U 1994

V 1995

W 1996

X 1997

Y 1998

In January 1999 there were several changes to the Hallmarking Act of 1973. Using the lion passant was no longer required but the offices still may use it. Instead, a numeric designation in an oval shows fineness (see examples below). Further, the date letters became standardized between offices.

800   958

925   999

A "Millennium Mark" was used at the assay offices from January 1, 1999 thru December 31, 2000. It was in a cruciform of the number 2000.

Z 1999

a 2000

BIRMINGHAM

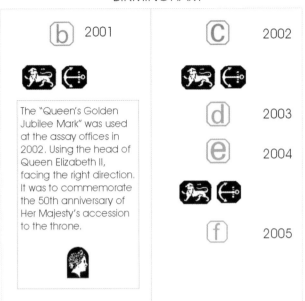

The "Queen's Golden Jubilee Mark" was used at the assay offices in 2002. Using the head of Queen Elizabeth II, facing the right direction. It was to commemorate the 50th anniversary of Her Majesty's accession to the throne.

191

1680	
1690	
circa 1690-1700	
1701	A
1702	B
1703	C
1704	D
1705	E
1706	F
1707	G
1708	H
1709	I
1710	K
1711	L
1712	M
1713	N
1714	O

1715	P
1716	Q
1717	R
1718	S
1719	T
1720	U
1721	V
1722	W
1723	X
1724	Y
1725	Z
1726	A
1727	B
1728	C
1729	D
1730	E

1731	F
1732	G
1733	H
1734	J
1735	K
1736	L
1737	M
1738	N
1739	O
1740	P
1741	Q
1742	R
1743	S
1744	T
1745	U
1746	V
1747	W
1748	X

Y	1749	P	1765	f	1781
Y	1749	Q	1766	g	1782
Z	1750	R	1767	h	1783
a	1751	S	1768	i	1784
b	1752	T	1769	k	1785
c	1753	T	1770	l	1786
d	1754	U	1771	m	1787
e	1755	V	1772	n	1788
f	1756	W	1773	o	1789
G	1757	X	1774	p	1790
h	1758	Y	1775	q	1791
i	1759	a	1776	r	1792
k	1760	b	1777	s	1793
l	1761	c	1778	t	1794
m	1762	d	1779	u	1795
n	1763	e	1780	v	1796
o	1764				

193

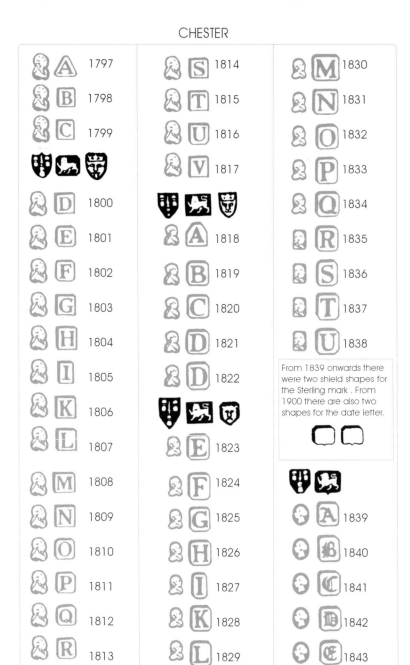

A 1797	S 1814	M 1830
B 1798	T 1815	N 1831
C 1799	U 1816	O 1832
	V 1817	P 1833
D 1800	A 1818	Q 1834
E 1801	B 1819	R 1835
F 1802	C 1820	S 1836
G 1803	D 1821	T 1837
H 1804	D 1822	U 1838
I 1805		
K 1806	E 1823	From 1839 onwards there were two shield shapes for the Sterling mark . From 1900 there are also two shapes for the date letter.
L 1807	F 1824	
M 1808	G 1825	
N 1809	H 1826	A 1839
O 1810	I 1827	B 1840
P 1811	K 1828	C 1841
Q 1812	L 1829	D 1842
R 1813		E 1843

1844	
1845	
1846	
1847	
1848	
1849	
1850	
1851	
1852	
1853	
1854	
1855	
1856	
1857	
1858	
1859	
1860	
1861	

1862
1863

1864
1865
1866
1867
1868
1869
1870
1871
1872
1873
1874
1875
1876
1877
1878

1879
1880
1881
1882
1883

1884
1885
1886
1887
1888
1889

1890
1891
1892
1893
1894

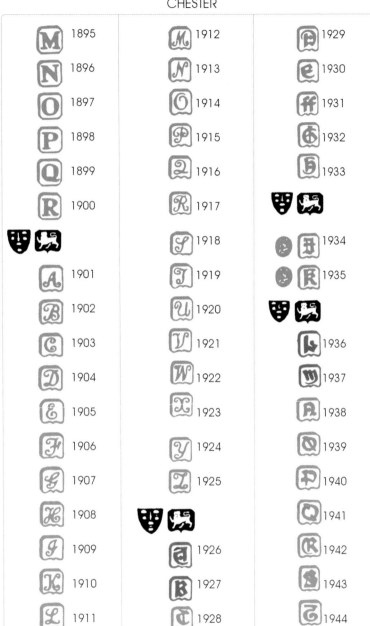

1895	1912	1929
1896	1913	1930
1897	1914	1931
1898	1915	1932
1899	1916	1933
1900	1917	
	1918	1934
1901	1919	1935
1902	1920	
1903	1921	1936
1904	1922	1937
1905	1923	1938
1906	1924	1939
1907	1925	1940
1908		1941
1909	1926	1942
1910	1927	1943
1911	1928	1944

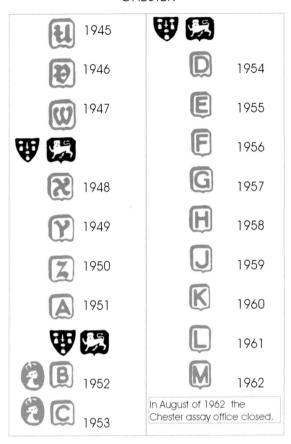

1945	1954
1946	1955
1947	1956
1948	1957
1949	1958
1950	1959
1951	1960
1952	1961
1953	1962

In August of 1962 the Chester assay office closed.

A 1638	
B 1639	
C 1640	
D 1641	
E 1642	
F 1643	
G 1644	
H 1645	
I 1646	
K 1647	
L 1648	
M 1649	
N 1650	
O 1651	
P 1652	
Q 1653	

R 1654	
S 1655	
T 1656	
U 1657	
a 1658	
b 1659	
c 1660	
d 1661	
e 1662	
f 1663	
g 1664	
h 1665	
i 1666	
k 1667	
l 1668	
m 1669	

n 1670	
o 1671	
p 1672	
q 1673	
r 1674	
s 1675	
t 1676	
u 1677	
A 1678	
B 1679	
C 1680	
D 1681	
E 1682	
F 1683-1684	
G 1685-1687	
H 1688-1693	

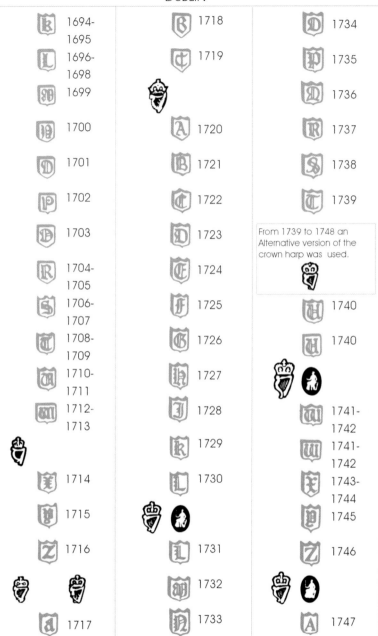

1694-1695	1718	1734
1696-1698	1719	1735
1699		1736
1700	1720	1737
1701	1721	1738
1702	1722	1739
1703	1723	
1704-1705	1724	From 1739 to 1748 an Alternative version of the crown harp was used.
1706-1707	1725	
1708-1709	1726	1740
1710-1711	1727	1740
1712-1713	1728	
	1729	1741-1742
1714	1730	1741-1742
1715		1743-1744
1716	1731	1745
	1732	1746
1717	1733	1747

B 1748	**P** 1763	**F** 1778
C 1749	**Q** 1764	**G** 1779
D 1750	**R** 1765	**H** 1780
E 1751	**S** 1766	**I** 1781
E 1751		**K** 1782
F 1752	**T** 1767	**L** 1783
	U 1768	**M** 1784
	W 1769	**N** 1785
	X 1770	**O** 1786
G 1753	**Y** 1771	
H 1754	**Z** 1772	**P** 1787
I 1757		**Q** 1788
K 1758	**A** 1773	**R** 1789
L 1759	**B** 1774	**S** 1790
	C 1775	**T** 1791
M 1760		**U** 1792
N 1761	**D** 1776	
O 1762	**E** 1777	**W** 1793

From 1751 to 1752 an alternative version of Hibernia was used.

X 1794	1810	F 1826
Y 1795	P 1811	
Z 1796	Q 1812	G 1827
	R 1813	
A 1797	S 1814	H 1828
B 1798	T 1815	
C 1799	U 1816	I 1829
D 1800	W 1817	
E 1801	X 1818	K 1830
F 1802	Y 1819	
G 1803	Z 1820	L 1831
H 1804		M 1832
I 1805	A 1821	
K 1806	B 1822	N 1833
L 1807	C 1823	
M 1808	D 1824	O 1834
N 1809	E 1825	P 1835
	e 1825	Q 1836

℞ 1837	d 1849	S 1863
S 1838	e 1850	
	f 1851	t 1864
T 1839	f 1851	u 1865
U 1840	g 1852	V 1866
V 1841	g 1852	W 1867
	h 1853	X 1868
W 1842	h 1853	Y 1869
X 1843	j 1854	Z 1870
Y 1844	k 1855	A 1871
	l 1856	B 1872
Z 1845	m 1857	C 1873
	n 1858	D 1874
a 1846	o 1859	E 1875
b 1847	p 1860	F 1876
c 1848	Q 1861	G 1877
	r 1862	H 1878

🛡Ⓘ	1879	Ⓐ	1896	Ⓣ	1914
🛡Ⓚ	1880	Ⓑ	1897	Ⓤ	1915
🛡Ⓛ	1881	Ⓒ	1898	🖤 🖤	
🛡Ⓜ	1882	Ⓓ	1899	Ⓐ	1916
🛡Ⓝ	1883	Ⓔ	1900	Ⓑ	1917
🛡Ⓞ	1884	Ⓕ	1901	Ⓒ	1918
🛡Ⓟ	1885	Ⓖ	1902	Ⓓ	1919
🛡Ⓠ	1886	Ⓗ	1903	Ⓔ	1920
🛡Ⓡ	1887	Ⓘ	1904	Ⓕ	1921
🛡Ⓢ	1888	Ⓚ	1905	Ⓢ	1922
🛡Ⓣ	1889	Ⓛ	1906	Ⓗ	1923
🛡Ⓤ	1890	Ⓜ	1907	Ⓘ	1924
Ⓥ	1891	Ⓐ	1908	Ⓚ	1925
Ⓦ	1892	Ⓞ	1909	Ⓛ	1926
Ⓧ	1893	Ⓟ	1910	Ⓜ	1927
Ⓨ	1894	Ⓠ	1911	Ⓝ	1928
Ⓩ	1895	Ⓡ	1912	Ⓞ	1929
🖤 🖤		Ⓢ	1913	Ⓟ	1930-1931

The date letter was changed prior to 1931 on June 1. Starting in 1932 all date letters were changed on January 1 of that year. This started with the Q.

Q	1932
R	1933
S	1934
T	1935
U	1936

V 1937
W 1938
X 1939
Y 1940
Z 1941

A 1942
B 1943
C 1944

D 1945
E 1946
F 1947
G 1948
H 1949
I 1950
J 1951
K 1952
L 1953
M 1954

N 1955
O 1956
P 1957
Q 1958
R 1959
S 1960
T 1961

U 1962
V 1963
W 1964
X 1965

Y 1966

A special mark the, "Sword of Light", was used to commemorate the 50th anniversary of the 1916 Rising, in 1966.

Z 1967

a 1968
b 1969
c 1970
d 1971
e 1972

1973

A special mark was used in 1973 showing the Gleninsheen Collar, this was to commemorate Ireland's entry into the EEC.

 1974

 1975

1976

1977

1978

1979

1980

1981

1982

1983

1984

1985

1986

 1987

In 1987 a special shield was used to commemorate the Goldsmiths' Company of Dublin's 350th anniversary.

 1988

In 1988 a special mark was used for the Dublin City millennium year commemorative.

1989

1990

1991

1992

1993

1994

1995

1996

1997

 1998

A "Millennium Mark" was used at the Dublin assay office from July 1, 1999 thru December 31, 2000. It was formed from the number 2 and the letter M.

1999

2000

2001

2002

1556	1643	1688
1563	1644	1689
1565	1649	1690
1575	1651	1691
1576	1660	1692
1577	1665	1693
1585	1669	1694
1591	1663-1681	1695
1598	1675	1696
1609		
1611	1681	1697
1617		
1617	1682	1698
1613-1621	1683	1699
1616-1635	1684	1700
1637	1685	1701
1640	1686	
1642	1687	1702

1703	N 1717	A 1730
1704	🏰 EP	B 1731
🏰 P	O 1718	C 1732
A 1705	P 1719	D 1733
B 1706	P 1719	E 1734
🏰 EP	🏰 EP	F 1735
C 1707	q 1720	G 1736
D 1708	R 1721	K 1737
E 1709	S 1722	J 1738
F 1710	T 1723	K 1739
G 1711	U 1724	🏰 GED
🏰 EP	V 1725	L 1740
H 1712	V 1725	M 1741
I 1713	W 1726	🏰 E·L
🏰 EP	X 1727	N 1742
K 1714	Y 1728	O 1743
L 1715	Z 1729	🏰 HG
M 1716	🏰 AU	P 1744

1745		1760		1774	
1746		1761		1775	
HG		1762		1776	
1747			1763	1777	
1748		1763		1778	
1749		1764		1779	
1750		1765			
1751		1766		1780	
1752		1767		1781	
1753		1768		1782	
1754		1769		1783	
HG		1770		1784	
1755		1771		1785	
1756				1786-1787	
1757				1788	
1758				1789	
		1772		1789	
1759		1773		1790	

Circa 1771 alternative town marks.

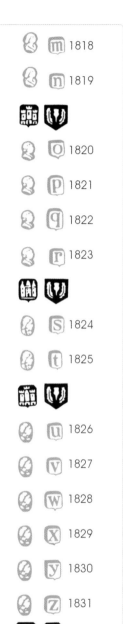

L 1791	X 1803	m 1818
M 1792	Y 1804	n 1819
N 1793	Z 1805	
N 1793		O 1820
O 1794	a 1806	P 1821
O 1794	b 1807	q 1822
P 1795	c 1808	r 1823
Q 1796		
	d 1809	S 1824
R 1797	e 1810	t 1825
R 1797	f 1811	
S 1798	g 1812	u 1826
		v 1827
T 1799	h 1813	w 1828
U 1800	i 1814	X 1829
V 1801	j 1815	y 1830
	k 1816	Z 1831
W 1802	l 1817	

	A	1832		T	1850		L	1867
	B	1833		H	1851		M	1868
	C	1834		U	1852		N	1869
	D	1835		W	1853		O	1870
	E	1836		X	1854		P	1871
	F	1837		Y	1855		Q	1872
	G	1838		Z	1856		R	1873
	H	1839					S	1874
	J	1840		A	1857		T	1875
	K	1841		B	1858		U	1876
	L	1842		C	1859		V	1877
	M	1843		D	1860		W	1878
	N	1844		E	1861		X	1879
	O	1845		F	1862		Y	1880
	P	1846		G	1863		Z	1881
	Q	1847		H	1864			
	R	1848		I	1865		a	1882
	S	1849		K	1866		b	1883

⊛ ⓒ 1884	ⓜ 1902	ⓞ 1919
⊛ ⓓ 1885	ⓡ 1903	ⓟ 1920
⊛ ⓔ 1886	ⓤ 1904	ⓠ 1921
⊛ ⓕ 1887	③ 1905	ⓡ 1922
⊛ ⓖ 1888		ⓢ 1923
⊛ ⓗ 1889	Ⓐ 1906	ⓣ 1924
⊛ ⓘ 1890	Ⓑ 1907	ⓤ 1925
ⓚ 1891	Ⓒ 1908	Ⓥ 1926
ⓛ 1892	Ⓓ 1909	Ⓦ 1927
ⓜ 1893	Ⓔ 1910	Ⓧ 1928
ⓝ 1894	Ⓕ 1911	Ⓨ 1929
ⓞ 1895	Ⓖ 1912	Ⓩ 1930
ⓟ 1896	Ⓗ 1913	
ⓠ 1897	Ⓘ 1914	Ⓐ 1931
ⓡ 1898	Ⓚ 1915	Ⓑ 1932
ⓢ 1899	Ⓛ 1916	Ⓒ 1933
ⓣ 1900	Ⓜ 1917	
ⓤ 1901	Ⓝ 1918	⊛ Ⓓ 1934

1935	1951	1966
		1967
1936	1952	1968
1937	1953	1969
1938		1970
	1954	1971
1939	1955	1972
1940		1973-1974
1941	1956	1975
1942	1957	1976
1943	1958	
1944	1959	1977
1945	1960	
1946	1961	1978
1947	1962	1979
1948	1963	1980
1949	1964	1981
1950	1965	

ℋ	1982
𝑔	1983
𝐾	1984
ℒ	1985
𝑀	1986
𝑁	1987
𝑂	1988
𝑃	1989
𝑄	1990
𝑅	1991
𝑆	1992
𝑇	1993
𝑈	1994
𝑉	1995
𝑊	1996
𝑋	1997
𝑦	1998

In January 1999 there were several changes to the Hallmarking Act of 1973. Using the lion passant was no longer required but the offices still may use it. Instead, a numeric designation in an oval shows fineness (see examples below). Further, the date letters became standardized between offices.

800 **958**

925 **999**

A "Millennium Mark" was used at the assay offices from January 1, 1999 thru December 31, 2000. It was in a cruciform of the number 2000.

𝑍	1999
𝑎	2000
𝑏	2001

The "Queen's Golden Jubilee Mark" was used at the assay offices in 2002. Using the head of Queen Elizabeth II, facing the right direction. It was to commemorate the 50th anniversary of Her Majesty's accession to the throne.

𝐶	2002
𝑑	2003
𝑒	2004
𝑓	2005

X IONS	c1570
I n	c1571
X X	c1575
X	c1580
X	1585

Around 1630 in Exeter, various town marks were used.

X	c1635-1675
X	c1635-1675
X	c1680
X	c1690
X	c1690
X	c1698
A	1701
B	1702
C	1703
D	1704
E	1705

F	1706
G	1707
H	1708
I	1709
K	1710
L	1711
M	1712
N	1713
O	1714
P	1715
Q	1716
R	1717
S	1718
T	1719
V	1720
W	1721

X	1722
Y	1723
Z	1724
a	1725
b	1726
c	1727
d	1728
e	1729
f	1730
g	1731
h	1732
i	1733
k	1734
l	1735
m	1736
n	1737
o	1738

p	1739	H	1756	A	1773
q	1740	I	1757	B	1774
r	1741	K	1758	C	1775
s	1742	L	1759	D	1776
t	1743	M	1760	E	1777
u	1744	N	1761		
w	1745	O	1762	F	1778
x	1746	P	1763	G	1779
y	1747	Q	1764	H	1780
z	1748	R	1765	I	1781-1782
		S	1766	K	1783
A	1749	T	1767	L	1784
B	1750	U	1768	M	1785
C	1751	W	1769	N	1786
D	1752	X	1770	O	1787
E	1753	Y	1771	P	1788
F	1754	Z	1772	q	1789
G	1755			r	1790

p 1791	L 1807	h 1824
t 1792	M 1808	i 1825
u 1793	N 1809	k 1826
W 1794	O 1810	l 1827
X 1795	P 1811	m 1828
y 1796	Q 1812	n 1829
	R 1813	o 1830
A 1797	S 1814	
B 1798	T 1815	P 1831
C 1799	U 1816	q 1832
D 1800		
E 1801	a 1817	r 1833
F 1802	b 1818	s 1834
G 1803	c 1819	t 1835
H 1804	d 1820	u 1836
	e 1821	
I 1805	f 1822	A 1837
K 1806	g 1823	B 1838

1839

 1840

 1841

 1842

 1843

 1844

 1845

 1846

 1847

 1848

1849

1850

1851

1852

1853

1854

 1855

 1856

 1857

 1858

 1859

 1860

 1861

 1862

 1863

 1864

 1865

 1866

 1867

 1868

1869

1870

1871

 1872

 1873

 1874

 1875

 1876

 1877

 1878

 1879

 1880

 1881

1882

In 1883 the Exeter assay office closed.

Between 1681 thru 1709 date letters were used then discontinued until 1819.

Up to 1784 the maker's mark was stamped on both sides of the Glasgow town mark.

 a 1681

 C 1683

 e 1685

 h 1689

 K 1690

 O 1694

 Q 1696

 S 1698

 t 1699

 U 1700

 v 1701

 y 1704

 z 1705

 B circa 1707

 D circa 1709

 circa 1717

It is believed that the letter S was used as a Sterling mark.

 S circa 1728

 S circa 1734

 S circa 1743

 S circa 1747

 S circa 1756

 circa 1757

 S circa 1758

 E circa 1763

 S circa 1773

 S circa 1773

 O circa 1776

 S circa 1780

 S circa 1781

 S circa 1783

 S circa 1784

 1811

 A 1819

 B 1820

 C 1821

 D 1822

 E 1823

 F 1824

 G 1825

 H 1826

 I 1827

 J 1828

 K 1829

 L 1830

 M 1831

 N 1832

O	1833	
P	1834	
Q	1835	
R	1836	
S	1837	
T	1838	
U	1839	
V	1840	
W	1841	
X	1842	
Y	1843	
Z	1844	
A	1845	
B	1846	
C	1847	
D	1848	
E	1849	
F	1850	
G	1851	
H	1852	
I	1853	
J	1854	
K	1855	
L	1856	
M	1857	
N	1858	
O	1859	
P	1860	
Q	1861	
R	1862	
S	1863	
T	1864	
U	1865	
V	1866	
W	1867	
X	1868	
Y	1869	
Z	1870	
A	1871	
B	1872	
C	1873	
D	1874	
E	1875	
F	1876	
G	1877	
H	1878	
I	1879	
J	1880	
K	1881	
L	1882	

M 1883	D 1900	U 1917
N 1884	E 1901	V 1918
O 1885	F 1902	W 1919
P 1886	G 1903	X 1920
Q 1887	H 1904	Y 1921
R 1888	I 1905	Z 1922
S 1889	J 1906	
T 1890	K 1907	a 1923
U 1891	L 1908	b 1924
V 1892	M 1909	c 1925
W 1893	N 1910	d 1926
X 1894	O 1911	e 1927
Y 1895	P 1912	f 1928
Z 1896	Q 1913	g 1929
		h 1930
A 1897	R 1914	i 1931
B 1898	S 1915	j 1932
C 1899	T 1916	k 1933

1949
1934
1935
1936
1937
1938
1939
1940
1941
1942
1943
1944
1945
1946
1947
1948
1950
1951
1952
1953
1954
1955
1956
1957
1958
1959
1960
1961
1962
1963

In 1964 the assay office at Glasgow closed.

G 1544	S 1555	I 1568
	T 1556	m 1569
H 1545		n 1570
I 1546	V 1557	O 1571
K 1547		p 1572
	a 1558	q 1573
L 1548	b 1559	r 1574
M 1549	C 1560	s† 1575
	C 1560	s 1575
N 1550	D 1561	t 1576
		u 1577
O 1551	e 1562	
O 1551	F 1563	A 1578
	g 1564	B 1579
P 1552	h 1565	C 1580
Q 1553	l 1566	D 1581
R 1554	k 1567	E 1582
	k 1567	F 1583

G 1584	D 1600	🛡️🦁
H 1585	D 1601	a 1618
I 1586	E 1602	b 1619
K 1587	F 1603	c 1620
L 1588	G 1604	d 1621
M 1589	h 1605	e 1622
N 1590	I 1606	f 1623
O 1591	K 1607	g 1624
👑🦁	L 1608	h 1625
P 1592	m 1609	i 1626
Q 1593	n 1610	k 1627
R 1594	O 1611	l 1628
S 1595	P 1612	m 1629
T 1596	Q 1613	n 1630
V 1597	R 1614	O 1631
👑🦁	S 1615	p 1632
A 1598	T 1616	q 1633
B 1599	V 1617	r 1634

1635
1636
1637

1638
1639
1640
1641
1642
1643
1644
1645
1646

1647
1648
1649
1650

1651
1652
1653
1654
1655
1656
1657

1658
1659
1660
1661
1662
1663
1664
1665
1666
1667

1668
1669
1670
1671
1672
1672
1673
1674
1675
1676
1677

1678
1679

1680
1681

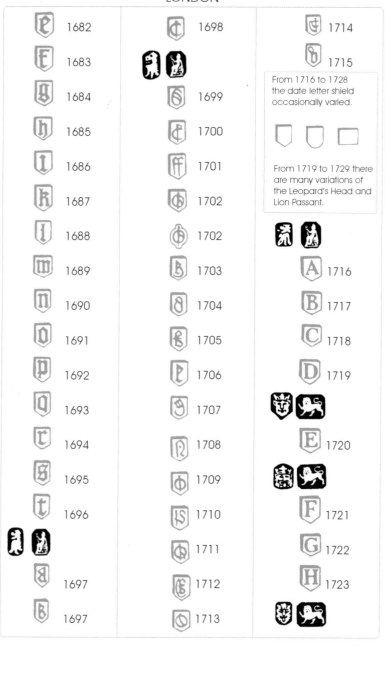

1682	1698	1714
1683		1715
1684	1699	From 1716 to 1728 the date letter shield occasionally varied.
1685	1700	
1686	1701	From 1719 to 1729 there are many variations of the Leopard's Head and Lion Passant.
1687	1702	
1688	1702	1716
1689	1703	1717
1690	1704	1718
1691	1705	1719
1692	1706	
1693	1707	1720
1694	1708	
1695	1709	1721
1696	1710	1722
	1711	1723
1697	1712	
1697	1713	

I	1724	d	1739	t	1754
K	1725	(crown) (lion)		u	1755
(head) (lion)		d	1739	(crown) (lion)	
L	1726	e	1740	A	1756
M	1727	f	1741	B	1757
N	1728	g	1742	C	1758
(crown) (lion)		h	1743	D	1759
O	1729	i	1744	E	1760
P	1730	k	1745	F	1761
Q	1731	l	1746	G	1762
R	1732	m	1747	H	1763
S	1733	n	1748	J	1764
T	1734	o	1749	k	1765
V	1735	p	1750	L	1766
(crown) (lion)		(crown) (lion)		M	1767
a	1736	q	1751	N	1768
b	1737	r	1752	O	1769
C	1738	ſ	1753	P	1770

LONDON

 1771

 1772

 1773

 1774

1774

1775

 or

From 1776 to 1795 two shield shapes are found.

From 1776 to 1795 a shield with no point was used on some small articles.

 1776

 1777

1778

1779

 1780

 1781

 1782

1783

 1784

 1785

 1786

 1787

 1788

 1789

 1790

 1791

 1792

 1793

 1794

 1795

 1796

  1797

 1798

 1799

 1800

 1801

 1802

 1803

 1804

 1805

 1806

 1807

 1808

 1809

 1820

 1811

 1812

 1813

 1814

U	1815		q	1831		M	1848
			r	1832		O	1849
a	1816		s	1833		P	1850
b	1817		t	1834		Q	1851
c	1818		u	1835		R	1852
d	1819					S	1853
e	1820		A	1836		T	1854
f	1821		B	1837		U	1855
g	1822		C	1838		a	1856
h	1823		D	1839		b	1857
i	1824		E	1840		c	1858
k	1825		F	1841		d	1859
l	1826		G	1842		e	1860
m	1827		H	1843		f	1861
n	1828		J	1844		g	1862
o	1829		K	1845		h	1863
p	1830		L	1846		i	1864
			M	1847			

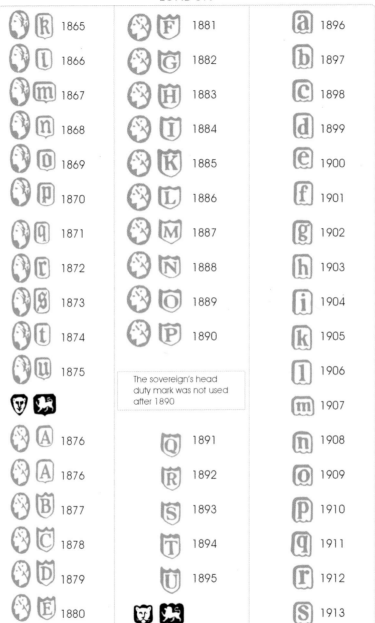

R 1865	F 1881	a 1896
l 1866	G 1882	b 1897
m 1867	H 1883	c 1898
n 1868	I 1884	d 1899
o 1869	K 1885	e 1900
p 1870	L 1886	f 1901
q 1871	M 1887	g 1902
r 1872	N 1888	h 1903
s 1873	O 1889	i 1904
t 1874	P 1890	k 1905
u 1875		l 1906
	The sovereign's head duty mark was not used after 1890	m 1907
A 1876	Q 1891	n 1908
A 1876	R 1892	o 1909
B 1877	S 1893	p 1910
C 1878	T 1894	q 1911
D 1879	U 1895	r 1912
E 1880		s 1913

t	1914	g	1931	M	1947
u	1915	r	1932	N	1948
		s	1933	O	1949
a	1916			P	1950
b	1917	t	1934	Q	1951
c	1918	u	1935		
d	1919			R	1952
e	1920	A	1936	S	1953
f	1921	B	1937		
g	1922	C	1938	T	1954
h	1923	D	1939	U	1955
i	1924	E	1940		
k	1925	F	1941	a	1956
l	1926	G	1942	b	1957
m	1927	H	1943	c	1958
n	1928	I	1944	d	1959
o	1929	K	1945	e	1960
p	1930	L	1946	f	1961

g 1962

h 1963

i 1964

k 1965

l 1966

m 1967

n 1968

o 1969

p 1970

q 1971

r 1972

s 1973

t 1974

In compliance with the Hallmarking act of 1973, A new letter sequence began on January 1, 1975.

A 1975

B 1976

C 1977

D 1978

E 1979

F 1980

G 1981

H 1982

I 1983

K 1984

L 1985

M 1986

N 1987

O 1988

P 1989

Q 1990

R 1991

S 1992

T 1993

U 1994

V 1995

W 1996

X 1997

Y 1998

In January 1999 there were several changes to the Hallmarking Act of 1973. Using the lion passant was no longer required but the offices still may use it. Instead, a numeric designation in an oval shows fineness (see examples below). Further, the date letters became standardized between offices.

 800   **958**

925   **999**

A "Millennium Mark" was used at the assay offices from January 1, 1999 thru December 31, 2000. It was in a cruciform of the number 2000.

Z 1999

2000

 2001

The "Queen's Golden Jubilee Mark" was used at the assay offices in 2002. Using the head of Queen Elizabeth II, facing the right direction. It was to commemorate the 50th anniversary of Her Majesty's accession to the throne.

 2002

 2003

 2004

 2005

NEWCASTLE

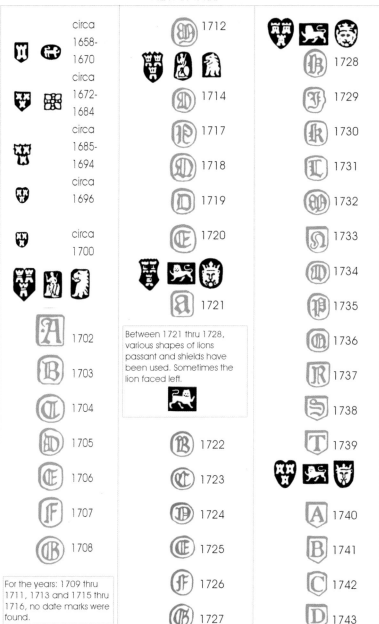

circa 1658-1670

circa 1672-1684

circa 1685-1694

circa 1696

circa 1700

1702
1703
1704
1705
1706
1707
1708

For the years: 1709 thru 1711, 1713 and 1715 thru 1716, no date marks were found.

1712

1714
1717
1718
1719
1720

1721

Between 1721 thru 1728, various shapes of lions passant and shields have been used. Sometimes the lion faced left.

1722
1723
1724
1725
1726
1727

1728
1729
1730
1731
1732
1733
1734
1735
1736
1737
1738
1739

1740
1741
1742
1743

E	1744	6	1769		U	1786
F	1745	D	1770		W	1787
G	1746	E	1771		X	1788
H	1747	F	1772		Y	1789
I	1748	G	1773		Z	1790
K	1749	H	1774			
L	1750	I	1775		A	1791
M	1751	K	1776		B	1792
N	1752	L	1777		C	1793
O	1753	M	1778		D	1794
P	1754				E	1795
Q	1755	N	1779		F	1796
R	1756	O	1780		G	1797
S	1757	P	1781		H	1798
S	1758	Q	1782		I	1799
		R	1783			
A	1759	S	1784		A	1791
B	1760-1768	T	1785		B	1792

234

C	1793	U	1810	N	1827
D	1794	W	1811	O	1828
E	1795	X	1812	P	1829
F	1796	Y	1813	Q	1830
G	1797	Z	1814	R	1831
H	1798			S	1832
I	1799	A	1815	T	1833
		B	1816	U	1834
K	1800	C	1817	W	1835
L	1801	D	1818	X	1836
M	1802	E	1819	Y	1837
N	1803	F	1820	Z	1838
O	1804	G	1821		
P	1805	H	1822	A	1839
Q	1806	I	1823	B	1840
R	1807	K	1824	C	1841
S	1808	L	1825	D	1842
T	1809	M	1826	E	1843

F 1844	X 1861
G 1845	Y 1862
	Z 1863
H 1846	
I 1847	a 1864
J 1848	b 1865
K 1849	c 1866
L 1850	d 1867
M 1851	e 1868
N 1852	f 1869
O 1853	g 1870
P 1854	h 1871
Q 1855	i 1872
R 1856	k 1873
S 1857	l 1874
T 1858	m 1875
U 1859	n 1876
W 1860	o 1877

p 1878
q 1879
r 1880
s 1881
t 1882
u 1883

In 1884 the Newcastle assay office closed.

A	1565
B	1566
C	1567
D	1568
E	1569
F	1570
G	1571
I	1573
K	1574
P	1579
	c1590
	c1595
	c1600
	c1610
	c1620

Between 1624 thru 1643 several versions of the town marks (see below) were used.

A	1624
B	1625
C	1626
D	1627
E	1628
F	1629
G	1630
H	1631
I	1632
K	1633
L	1634
M	1635
N	1636
O	1637
P	1638
Q	1639
R	1640
S	1641

T	1642
V	1643
	c1645
	c1650
	c1655
	c1660
	c1665
	c1670
	c1675
	c1680
	c1685
a	1688
b	1689
d	1691
I	1696
K	1697

After 1701 very little silver was assayed at Norwich.

A 1701

237

From 1773 to 1779 these hallmarks were used for assay of large and small objects.

 1773

1774

1775

1776

1777

1778

1779

From 1780 to 1823 the crown and lion passant had slight variations.

From 1824 to 1843 the variation was the crown in the square shield.

1780

1781

1782

1783

1784

1785

1786

1787

1788

1789

1790

1791

1792

1793

1794

1795

1796

1797

From July 15, 1797 for nine months the king's head was stamped twice because the duty on silver was doubled.

1798
1799
1800
1801
1802
1803
1804
1805
1806
1807
1808
1809
1810
1811
1812
1813
1814
1815

T 1816		m 1834		H 1851			
X 1817		P 1835		I 1852			
I 1818		q 1836		K 1853			
V 1819		r 1837					
Q 1820		S 1838					
Y 1821		t 1839					
Z 1822		u 1840					
U 1823		V 1841					
a 1824		X 1842					
b 1825		Z 1843					
C 1826							
d 1827		A 1844					
e 1828		B 1845					
f 1829		C 1846					
g 1830		D 1847					
h 1831		E 1848					
k 1832		F 1849					
l 1833		G 1850					

From 1780 to 1853 the Sheffield assay office used the combined crown and date letters on small objects.

1780	
1781	
1782	
1783	
1784	
1785	
1786	
1787	
1788	
1789	
1790	
1791	

239

Date letter	Year	Date letter	Year	Date letter	Year
u	1792	L	1810	e	1828
O	1793	C	1811	f	1829
m	1794	D	1812	g	1830
q	1795	R	1813	h	1831
Z	1796	W	1814	k	1832
X	1797	O	1815	l	1833
V	1798	T	1816	E	1834
E	1799	X	1817	p	1835
N	1800	I	1818	q	1836
H	1801	V	1819	r	1837
M	1802	Q	1820	s	1838
F	1803	Y	1821	t	1839
G	1804	Z	1822	u	1840
B	1805	U	1823	v	1841
A	1806	a	1824	x	1842
S	1807	b	1825	z	1843
P	1808	c	1826	A	1844
K	1809	d	1827	B	1845

SHEFFIELD

C	1846	U	1862	L	1878
D	1847	V	1863	M	1879
E	1848	W	1864	N	1880
F	1849	X	1865	O	1881
G	1850	Y	1866	P	1882
H	1851	Z	1867	Q	1883
I	1852			R	1884
K	1853	A	1868	S	1885

In 1854 the Sheffield assay office returned to a single assay for large and small objects.

L	1854	B	1869	T	1886
M	1855	C	1870	U	1887
N	1856	D	1871	V	1888
O	1857	E	1872	W	1889
P	1858			X	1890
R	1859	F	1873	Y	1891
S	1860	G	1874	Z	1892
T	1861	H	1875		
		J	1876	a	1893
		K	1877	b	1894

© 1895	𝖞 1913	𝖓 1930
𝖉 1896	𝖜 1914	𝖔 1931
𝖊 1897	𝖝 1915	𝖕 1932
𝕰 1898	𝖞 1916	𝖖 1933
𝖌 1899	𝖟 1917	
𝖍 1990		𝖗 1934
𝖎 1901	𝖆 1918	𝖘 1935
𝖐 1902	𝖇 1919	
𝖑 1903	𝖈 1920	𝖙 1936
𝖒 1904	𝖉 1921	𝖚 1937
𝖓 1905	𝖊 1922	𝖛 1938
𝖔 1906	𝖋 1923	𝖜 1939
𝖕 1907	𝖌 1924	𝖝 1940
𝖖 1908	𝖍 1925	𝖞 1941
𝖗 1909	𝖎 1926	𝖟 1942
𝖘 1910	𝖐 1927	
𝖙 1911	𝖑 1928	𝖆 1943
𝖚 1912	𝖒 1929	𝖇 1944

C 1945	T 1961	
D 1946	U 1962	A 1975
E 1947	V 1963	B 1976
F 1948	W 1964	C 1977
G 1949	X 1965	
H 1950	Y 1966	D 1978
I 1951	Z 1967	E 1979
K 1952	A 1968	F 1980
L 1953	B 1969	G 1981
M 1954	C 1970	H 1982
N 1955	D 1971	I 1983
O 1956	E 1972	K 1984
P 1957		L 1985
Q 1958	F 1973	M 1986
R 1959	G 1974	N 1987
S 1960		O 1988
		P 1989

In 1973 to commemorate the Sheffield assay office bicentennial the 1773 date letter was used.

In complying with the Hallmarking Act of 1973, a new letter sequence was started on January 1, 1975.

1990

 1991

1992

1993

1994

1995

1996

1997

1998

A "Millennium Mark" was used at the assay offices from January 1, 1999 thru December 31, 2000. It was in a cruciform of the number 2000.

 1999

 2000

 2001

The "Queen's Golden Jubilee Mark" was used at the assay offices in 2002. Using the head of Queen Elizabeth II, facing the right direction. It was to commemorate the 50th anniversary of Her Majesty's accession to the throne.

In January 1999 there were several changes to the Hallmarking Act of 1973. Using the lion passant was no longer required but the offices still may use it. Instead, a numeric designation in an oval shows fineness (see examples below). Further, the date letters became standardized between offices.

 800   958

 925   999

 2002

2003

2004

2005

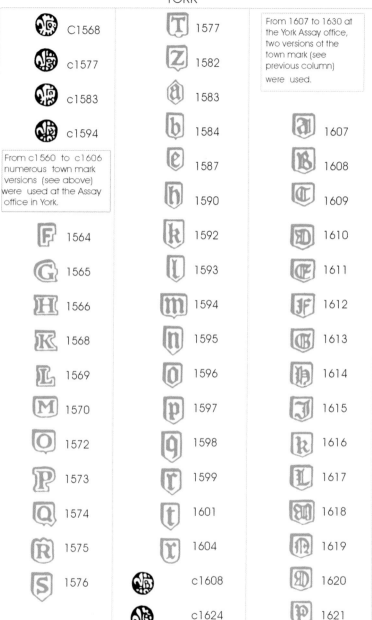

C1568

c1577

c1583

c1594

From c1560 to c1606 numerous town mark versions (see above) were used at the Assay office in York.

F 1564

G 1565

H 1566

K 1568

L 1569

M 1570

O 1572

P 1573

Q 1574

R 1575

S 1576

T 1577

Z 1582

a 1583

b 1584

e 1587

h 1590

k 1592

l 1593

m 1594

n 1595

o 1596

p 1597

q 1598

r 1599

t 1601

r 1604

c1608

c1624

From 1607 to 1630 at the York Assay office, two versions of the town mark (see previous column) were used.

a 1607

B 1608

C 1609

D 1610

E 1611

F 1612

G 1613

H 1614

J 1615

k 1616

L 1617

M 1618

N 1619

D 1620

P 1621

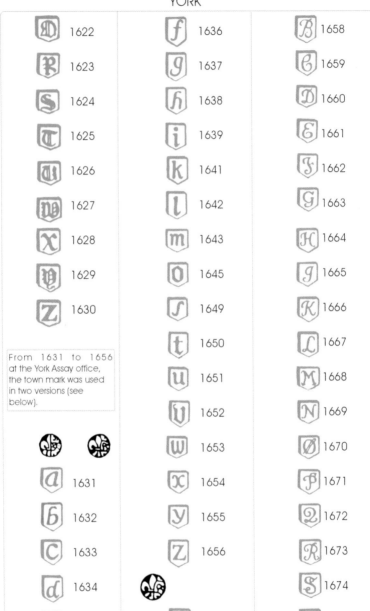

1622	1636	1658
1623	1637	1659
1624	1638	1660
1625	1639	1661
1626	1641	1662
1627	1642	1663
1628	1643	1664
1629	1645	1665
1630	1649	1666
	1650	1667
	1651	1668
	1652	1669
	1653	1670
1631	1654	1671
1632	1655	1672
1633	1656	1673
1634		1674
1635	1657	1675

From 1631 to 1656 at the York Assay office, the town mark was used in two versions (see below).

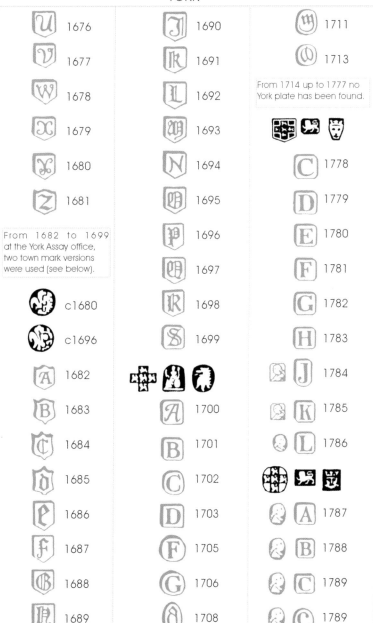

1676	1690	1711
1677	1691	1713
1678	1692	From 1714 up to 1777 no York plate has been found.
1679	1693	
1680	1694	1778
1681	1695	1779
From 1682 to 1699 at the York Assay office, two town mark versions were used (see below).	1696	1780
	1697	1781
c1680	1698	1782
c1696	1699	1783
1682		1784
1683	1700	1785
1684	1701	1786
1685	1702	
1686	1703	1787
1687	1705	1788
1688	1706	1789
1689	1708	1789

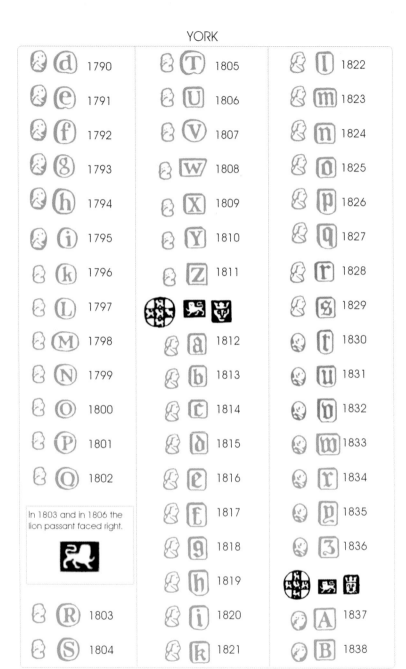

1790	1805	1822
1791	1806	1823
1792	1807	1824
1793	1808	1825
1794	1809	1826
1795	1810	1827
1796	1811	1828
1797		1829
1798	1812	1830
1799	1813	1831
1800	1814	1832
1801	1815	1833
1802	1816	1834
	1817	1835
	1818	1836
	1819	
	1820	1837
1803	1821	1838
1804		

In 1803 and in 1806 the lion passant faced right.

	C	1839
	D	1840
	E	1841
	F	1842
	G	1843
	H	1844
	I	1845
	K	1846
	L	1847
	M	1848
	N	1849
	O	1850
	P	1851
	Q	1852
	R	1853
	S	1854
	T	1855
	V	1856

In 1856 the York assay office closed.

United States

As a British colony, America was intended to provide raw materials to Great Britain. In exchange, England would have an outlet for finished goods, including silver flatware and hollowware. As such, England never established assay offices in the American Colonies.

In fact, no legal system of marking precious metals was adopted in the United States until the National Metal Stamping Act of 1906.

This law required that if a piece of silver is marked with the words "Sterling," it must be .925 fineness. If the piece is marked "coin," it must be .900 fineness. There is a common misconception that we stopped using coin silver after the civil war. The fact that the law provides for the use of the word "coin" implies that silversmiths continued to use the coin standard into the twentieth century.

Although Tiffany and Company changed to the Sterling standard in 1851 and Gorham changed in 1868, other manufacturers were slow to change.

In fact, retailers used silver content as a sales tool. If you could not afford Sterling, they offered things made of "coin" standard. In Chapter 5, Figure 5-20, we saw a page advertising coin silver napkin rings in the Clapp, Young and Company catalog of 1878.

Another picture from the same catalog shows a "solid silver" card case and tobacco box. (See Figure 7-168.) "Solid silver" could mean that the item was not silverplated.

Gold and silver items were marked as individual companies saw fit. There was no guarantee to the consumer. It posed a problem for reputable manufacturers and retailers, as dishonest merchants made the industry look bad. In those days, the federal government was hesitant to pass laws that could be viewed as conflicting with states' rights.

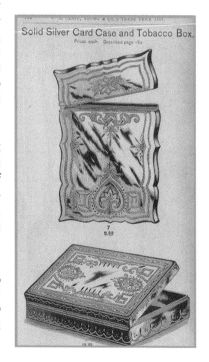

Not only were there no laws that guaranteed the fineness, but there was no system to provide a date of manufacture or assay. Some individual exceptions are shown below, but dating American silver becomes much more of an art than a science.

Figure 7-105: 1878 Clapp, Young and Company "solid silver" card case and tobacco box

For the most part, American silversmiths registered their marks and only changed them if the ownership changed. It leaves us to individually research the time period that a company may have been in business. Some companies used their own dating systems. Some had well documented name changes and policy changes that can also be useful for dating. They are listed here as a quick reference guide.

Gorham Corporation

1831 – Gorham and Webster
1837 – Gorham, Webster and Price
1841 – Jabez Gorham and Son
1850 – Gorham and Thurber
1852 – Gorham and Company
1863 – Gorham Manufacturing Company
1868 – Gorham dropped the coin standard and adopted the Sterling standard. Gorham began using the Lion, "G," and Anchor mark for sterling, with the lion facing right instead of left.
1868 to 1884 – Gorham adopted a letter code system to denote the year, beginning with "A" and ending with "Q."
1887 to 1933 – Gorham adopted a symbol system to denote the year.
1941 to present – Gorham adopted a geometric symbol to denote the decade, with a number inside to indicate the year; a square for the 1940s, a shield for the 1950s, etc.

**Figure 7-106:
Gorham maker's
marks**

**Figure 7-107: 1908
Gorham year mark**

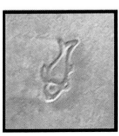

**Figure 7-108: 1912
Gorham year mark**

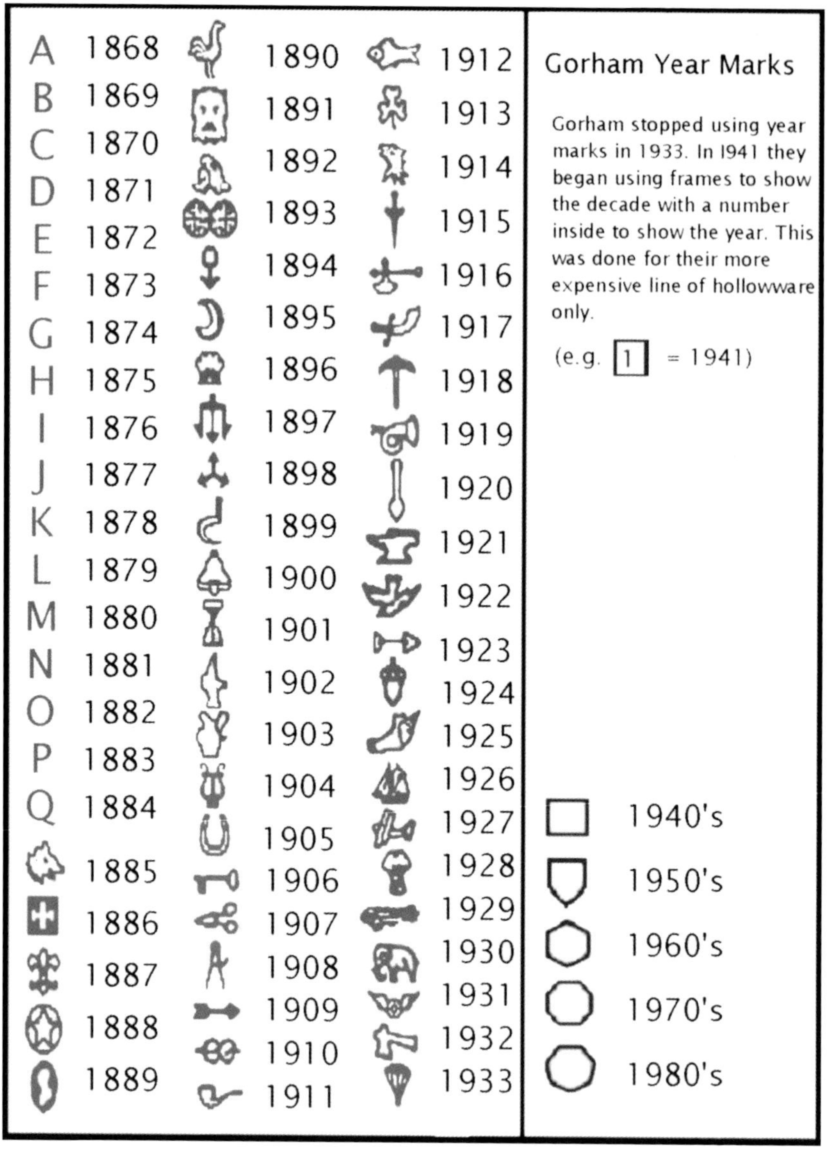
A 1868
B 1869
C 1870
D 1871
E 1872
F 1873
G 1874
H 1875
I 1876
J 1877
K 1878
L 1879
M 1880
N 1881
O 1882
P 1883
Q 1884
1885
1886
1887
1888
1889
1890
1891
1892
1893
1894
1895
1896
1897
1898
1899
1900
1901
1902
1903
1904
1905
1906
1907
1908
1909
1910
1911
1912
1913
1914
1915
1916
1917
1918
1919
1920
1921
1922
1923
1924
1925
1926
1927
1928
1929
1930
1931
1932
1933
Gorham Year Marks
Gorham stopped using year marks in 1933. In l941 they began using frames to show the decade with a number inside to show the year. This was done for their more expensive line of hollowware only.
(e.g. 1 = 1941)
1940's
1950's
1960's
1970's
1980's

Figure 7-109: Gorham year marks, 1868 through 1980s

Samuel Kirk and Son

1814 to 1830 – The company used Baltimore assay marks (discussed later in this chapter), along with their maker's marks.

1817 to 1820 – Kirk and Smith
1821 to 1846 – Samuel Kirk
1846 to 1861 – Samuel Kirk and Son
1861 to 1868 – Samuel Kirk and Sons
1868 to 1896 – Samuel Kirk and Son
1868 – Samuel Kirk and Son began to use the Sterling standard, denoted as .925.
1896 to 1924 – Samuel Kirk and Son Co.
1924 to present – Samuel Kirk and Son, Inc.
1925 to present –   The word "Sterling" appears on silver flatware and hollowware.
1979 – Samuel Kirk and Sons, Inc. was purchased by Stieff. The firm name was changed to Kirk Stieff Company.

Figure 7-110: S. Kirk and Son, company mark, 1896 to 1924

Tiffany and Company, Inc.

1837 – Founded as a fancy goods store, purchasing all silver from John C. Moore.
1852 – Tiffany, Young and Ellis
1851 – Tiffany began to use .925 fineness as its company standard, using the words "Sterling" along with its trademark.
1853 – Tiffany and Company
1868 – Tiffany and Company, Inc.
1868 – Tiffany trademark began to incorporate the initial of the incumbent company president.

Figure 7-111: Tiffany marks

Tuttle Silversmiths

1890 – Founded by Timothy Tuttle, using the Pine Tree Shilling Symbol.

1923 to present – Tuttle used a crescent with the initials of the United States President, along with the Pine Tree shilling mark.

> **1923 to 1929** – CC, Calvin Coolidge
> **1929 to 1933** – HH, Herbert Hoover
> **1933 to 1945** – FR, Franklin Roosevelt
> **1947 to 1953** – HT, Harry Truman
> **1953 to 1961** – DE, Dwight Eisenhower
> **1961 to 1963** – JFK, John F. Kennedy
> **1963 to 1969** – LBJ, Lyndon B. Johnson
> **1969 to 1974** – RMN, Richard M. Nixon
> **1974 to 1977** – GRF, Gerald Ford
> **1977 to 1981** – JEC, Jimmy Carter
> **1981 to 1989** – RWR, Ronald Regan
> **1989 to 1993** – GHB, George H. Bush
> **1993 to 2001** – WJC, William J. Clinton
> **2001 to present** – GWB, George W. Bush

1955 – Company was purchased by Wallace Silversmiths. On occasion, some contemporary pieces are not marked with President's initials.

Key Legislative Acts

Some key legislative acts aid in the dating of silver. They include Baltimore Assay Marks, the McKinley Tariff Act, and the National Gold and Silver Marking Act.

Baltimore Assay Marks

Starting in 1814, silver made in Baltimore, Maryland, was assayed and marked at a hall and identified by a date letter, referred to as a Dominical letter. The letters A to G represent the date of the first Sunday of the year. For example, if the first Sunday fell on January 2, the date letter for the year would be B. A leap year was represented by two Dominical letters.

This compulsory marking was discontinued in 1830. American silver bearing Baltimore assay marks commands a premium because of its rarity, provenance, and fineness guarantee.

254

**Figure 7-112: 1814
Baltimore assay mark**

The McKinley Tariff Act of 1890

Enacted in 1890, this tariff required that products imported into the United States be marked with the country of origin. This act required that imported items be marked in "legible English words."

The McKinley act was amended in 1894 to require that imports be marked with "the quantity of their contents" in "legible English words," along with the country of origin. This was probably an early attempt to require that the content of precious metals be marked. It was not very specific and probably did not carry much weight. However, it does suggest that you may see some imports marked with metal content before 1907.

The McKinley act was amended again in 1930. At this time, it required that "the *English name* of the country of origin" (italics added) be marked on imported items. It further empowered the Secretary of the Treasury to "determine the character of words and phrases or abbreviations thereof which shall be acceptable as indicating the country of origin."

We associate this revision of the McKinley act to be the point in time at which the words "made in" were required, although the term may have been in use before the law was amended in 1930.

The English enacted a similar marking requirement in 1881, requiring that the country of origin be marked on imported items. Therefore, a piece of silver marked with the country of origin can predate the McKinley Tariff Act by nine years.

National Gold and Silver Stamping Act of 1905

At the urging of industry leaders, the federal government passed a series of laws dealing with gold and silver marking.

The laws required that the words "Sterling" could not be marked on any article that was less that .925 fineness. This included the solder used to join the article together.

The word "coin" could not be marked on any article that was less than .900 fineness, again including the solder.

The laws also said that any mark used must be within a .004 tolerance of the mark used. This means that if the item is Sterling it could not be less than .921 fineness. Coin could not be less than .896 fineness.

Names like German silver, Brazil silver, Alaska silver, White silver, and nickel silver, all of which had no silver in them, could no longer be used. What this has given us, in a roundabout way, is a cut-off date for zero content silver items that used these names.

The law further required that if a <u>silverplated</u> item used words to indicate that it was Sterling or coin, there must be markings to disclose that the item was plated and not solid.

The law forbade the U.S. manufacture of items marked this way after February 21, 1905. It forbade the importation and transport of these items after June 13, 1907.

If you are interested in reading the entire code, you can find it under United States Codes, Title 15, Chapter 8, Sections 291 through 300.

Appendix

Kings and Rulers of England and France

United States Presidents

Vienna Hallmarking Convention

British Design Registry System

United States Utility and Design Patent Numbers

Weights, Measures and Conversions

Kings and Rulers

England

Tudor
Henry VIII	1509 - 1547
Edward VI	1547 - 1553
Mary	1553 - 1558
Elizabeth I	1558 - 1603

Stuart
James I	1603 - 1625
Charles	1625 - 1649

Protectorate
Cromwell	1649 - 1660
Charles II	1660 - 1685
James II	1685 - 1689
William and Mary	1689 - 1702
Anne	1702 - 1714

Hanover
George I	1714 - 1727
George II	1727 - 1760
George III	1760 - 1820
George IV	1820 - 1830
William IV	1830 - 1837
Victoria	1837 - 1901

Saxe-Coburg Gotha/ Windsor
Edward VII	1901 - 1910
George V	1910 - 1936
Edward VIII	1936
George VI	1936 - 1952
Elizabeth II	1952

France

Valois
Francois I	1515 - 1547
Henri II	1547 - 1559
Francois II	1559 - 1560
Charles IV	1560 - 1574

Bourbon
Henri IV	1589 - 1610
Louis XIII	1610 - 1643
Louis XIV	1643 - 1715
Philippe	1715 - 1723
Louis XV	1723 - 1774
Louis XVI	1774 - 1793

Revolution	1789 - 1795
Directoire	1795 - 1799
Consulate	1799 - 1804

Bonaparte
Napoleon I	1804 -1814
(first empire)	

Bourbon (Restoration)
Louis XVIII	1815 - 1824
Charles X	1824 - 1830

Orleans
Louis-Philippe	1830 - 1848

Second Empire	1848 - 1870
Napolean III	1851 - 1870

Third Republic	1871 - 1940

United States Presidents

George Washington	1789-1797
John Adams	1797-1801
Thomas Jefferson	1801-1809
James Madison	1809-1817
James Monroe	1817-1825
John Quincy Adams	1825-1829
Andrew Jackson	1829-1837
Martin Van Buren	1837-1841
William Henry Harrison	1841
John Tyler	1841-1845
James Knox Polk	1845-1849
Zachary Taylor	1849-1850
Millard Fillmore	1850-1853
Franklin Pierce	1853-1857
James Buchanan	1857-1861
Abraham Lincoln	1861-1865
Andrew Johnson	1865-1869
Ulysses Simpson Grant	1869-1877
Rutherford Birchard Hayes	1877-1881
James Abram Garfield	1881
Chester Alan Arthur	1881-1885
Grover Cleveland	1885-1889
Benjamin Harrison	1889-1893
Grover Cleveland	1893-1897
William McKinley	1897-1901
Theodore Roosevelt	1901-1909
William Howard Taft	1909-1913
Woodrow Wilson	1913-1921
Warren Gamaliel Harding	1921-1923
Calvin Coolidge	1923-1929
Herbert Clark Hoover	1929-1933
Franklin Delano Roosevelt	1933-1945
Harry S. Truman	1945-1953
Dwight David Eisenhower	1953-1961
John Fitzgerald Kennedy	1961-1963
Lyndon Baines Johnson	1963-1969
Richard Milhous Nixon	1969-1974
Gerald Rudolph Ford	1974-1977
Jimmy (James Earl) Carter	1977-1981
Ronald Reagan	1981-1989
George H.W. Bush	1989-1993
William Jefferson Clinton	1993-2001
George W. Bush	2001- to present

Vienna Hallmarking Convention

Silver marking has been practiced as a way to verify the content of precious metals. At the same time, marks from different countries can be difficult to understand and interpret. In an effort to help international trade, discussions between several countries began in the 1960s which led to an agreement signed in Vienna in 1972. The agreement went into effect in November of 1975.

Along with tolerance guidelines and marking requirements, the Hallmarking Convention created a series of marks, called *common control marks*, which could be recognized and accepted by member countries. This meant that precious metals marked with the common control marks did not have to be re-assayed when imported.

The first countries to adopt the common control marks were:

Austria
Finland
Norway
Portugal
Sweden
Switzerland
United Kingdom

By 2006, eight other countries agreed to the Hallmarking Convention guidelines.

Denmark
Hungary
Israel
The Czech Republic
The Netherlands
Latvia
Lithuania
Poland

Cyprus, Slovak Republic and the Ukraine are currently in the process of accepting the convention guidelines. The common control mark for silver is a scale inside a rectangle with cut corners. The fineness is represented in thousandths is shown below.

English Design Registry System

The Design Act of 1842 consolidated all earlier acts and simplified the process to register a design. A diamond-shaped mark was used to show the type of material registered . It also showed the month and year of registration and a parcel number. The Design Act protected the design for three years, although manufacturers continued to mark their wares long after the legal protection expired.

This act divided designs into categories based on the type of material used which included metal, wood, glass and ceramics as shown in Table 1 on the following page. At first, the year was shown under the substance, the month was on the left side of the diamond, the day of the month was on the right and the parcel number could be found at the bottom of the diamond.

The system was modified slightly in 1867 moving the day of the month to the top of the diamond, the year on the right, the month at the bottom and the parcel number on the left side.

This system remained in effect until 1883. Instead of using the diamond-shaped mark, the letters "Rd" proceeded a number, beginning with the number "1" in 1884 and continuing until 1989. In 1989 the beginning number in August changed to 2,000,000.

United States Patents Number System

United States patents date back to the 1790s, but the patent office was burned down during the war of 1812. The patent office reopened in 1836. The first number issued in 1836 was "1".

In 1843, the patent office began to issue design patents. The first number issued was "D1". Charts with utility and design patents are shown following the English system of registration.

English Design Registry Marks

1842 to 1883

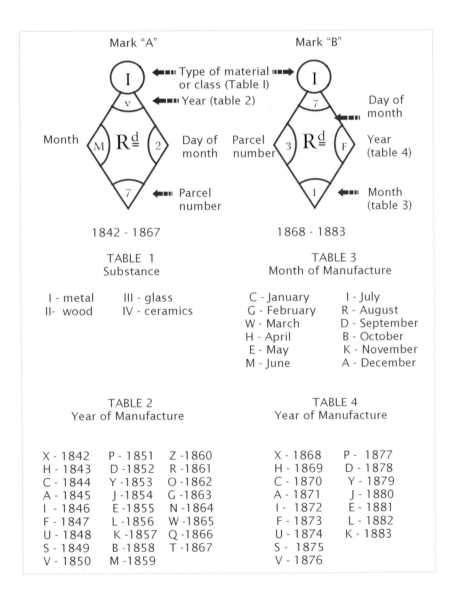

Mark "A" Mark "B"

← Type of material → or class (Table I)

← Year (table 2)

Month

Day of month

Parcel number

Parcel number

Day of month

Year (table 4)

Month (table 3)

1842 - 1867 1868 - 1883

TABLE 1
Substance

I - metal   III - glass
II- wood   IV - ceramics

TABLE 3
Month of Manufacture

C - January   I - July
G - February   R - August
W - March   D - September
H - April   B - October
E - May   K - November
M - June   A - December

TABLE 2
Year of Manufacture

X - 1842	P - 1851	Z -1860
H - 1843	D -1852	R -1861
C - 1844	Y -1853	O -1862
A - 1845	J -1854	G -1863
I - 1846	E -1855	N -1864
F - 1847	L -1856	W -1865
U - 1848	K -1857	Q -1866
S - 1849	B -1858	T -1867
V - 1850	M -1859	

TABLE 4
Year of Manufacture

X - 1868	P - 1877
H - 1869	D - 1878
C - 1870	Y - 1879
A - 1871	J - 1880
I - 1872	E - 1881
F - 1873	L - 1882
U - 1874	K - 1883
S - 1875	
V - 1876	

English Design Registry Numbers
1884 to 1995

Year	Number	Year	Number	Year	Number
1884	1	1922	687,144	1960	895,000
1885	19,754	1923	694,999	1961	899,914
1886	40,480	1924	702,671	1962	904,638
1887	64,520	1925	710,165	1963	909,364
1888	90,483	1926	718,057	1964	914,536
1889	116,648	1927	726,330	1965	919,607
1890	141,273	1928	734,370	1966	924,510
1891	163,767	1929	742,725	1967	929,335
1892	185,713	1930	751,160	1968	934,515
1893	205,240	1931	760,583	1969	939,875
1894	224,720	1932	769,670	1970	944,932
1895	246,975	1933	779,292	1971	950,046
1896	268,392	1934	789,019	1972	955,342
1897	291,241	1935	799,097	1973	960,708
1898	311,658	1936	808,794	1974	965,185
1899	331,707	1937	817,293	1975	969,249
1900	351,202	1938	825,231	1976	973,838
1901	368,154	1939	832,610	1977	978,426
1902	385,180	1940	837,520	1978	982,815
1903	403,200	1941	838,500	1979	987,910
1904	424,400	1942	839,230	1980	993,012
1905	447,800	1943	839,980	1981	998,302
1906	471,860	1944	841,040	1982	1,004,456
1907	493,900	1945	842,670	1983	1,010,583
1908	518,640	1946	845,550	1984	1,017,131
1909	535,170	1947	849,730	1985	1,024,174
1910	552,000	1948	853,260	1986	1,031,358
1911	574,817	1949	856,999	1987	1,039,055
1912	594,195	1950	860,854	1988	1,047,478
1913	612,431	1951	863,970	1989	1,056,076
1914	630,190	1952	866,280	July-89	1,061,406*
1915	644,935	1953	869,300	Aug-89	2,000,000
1916	653,521	1954	872,531	1990	2,003,720
1917	658,988	1955	876,067	1991	2,012,047
1918	662,872	1956	879,282	1992	2,019,933
1919	666,128	1957	882,949	1993	2,028,110
1920	673,750	1958	887,079	1994	2,036,116
1921	680,147	1959	891,665	1995	2,044,229

*Last number issued in the old numbering system

United States Utility and Design Patent Numbers 1836 to 1915

Issue Year	First Utility	First Design	Issue Year	First Utility	First Design
1836	1		1876	171,641	D8,884
1837	110		1877	185,813	D9,686
1838	546		1878	198,733	D10,385
1839	1,061		1879	211,078	D10,975
1840	1,465		1880	223,211	D11,567
1841	1,923		1881	236,137	D12,082
1842	2,413		1882	251,685	D12,647
1843	2,901	D 1	1883	269,820	D13,508
1844	3,395	D15	1884	291,016	D14,528
1845	3,873	D27	1885	310,163	D15,678
1846	4,348	D44	1886	333,494	D16,451
1847	4,914	D103	1887	355,291	D17,046
1848	5,409	D163	1888	375,720	D17,995
1849	5,993	D209	1889	395,305	D18,830
1850	6,981	D258	1890	418,665	D19,553
1851	7,865	D341	1891	443,987	D20,439
1852	8,622	D431	1892	466,315	D21,275
1853	9,512	D540	1893	488,976	D22,092
1854	10,358	D626	1894	511,744	D22,994
1855	12,117	D683	1895	531,619	D23,922
1856	14,009	D753	1896	552,502	D25,037
1857	16,324	D860	1897	574,369	D26,482
1858	19,010	D973	1898	596,467	D28,113
1859	22,477	D1,075	1899	616,871	D29,916
1860	26,642	D1,183	1900	640,167	D32,055
1861	31,005	D1,366	1901	664,827	D33,813
1862	34,045	D1,508	1902	690,385	D35,547
1863	37,266	D1,703	1903	717,521	D36,187
1864	41,047	D1,879	1904	748,567	D36,723
1865	45,685	D2,018	1905	778,834	D37,280
1866	51,784	D2,239	1906	808,618	D37,766
1867	60,658	D2,533	1907	839,799	D38,391
1868	72,959	D2,858	1908	875,679	D38,980
1869	85,503	D3,304	1909	908,436	D39,737
1870	98,460	D3,810	1910	945,010	D40,424
1871	110,617	D4,547	1911	980,178	D41,063
1872	122,304	D5,452	1912	1,013,095	D42,073
1873	134,504	D6,336	1913	1,049,326	D43,415
1874	146,120	D7,083	1914	1,083,267	D45,098
1875	158,350	D7,969	1915	1,123,212	D46,813

United States Utility and Design Patent Numbers 1915 to 1994

Issue Year	First Utility	First Design	Issue Year	First Utility	First Design
1916	1,166,419	D48,358	1955	2,698,434	D173,777
1917	1,210,389	D50,117	1956	2,728,913	D176,490
1918	1,251,458	D51,629	1957	2,775,762	D179,467
1919	1,290,027	D52,836	1958	2,818,567	D181,829
1920	1,326,899	D54,359	1959	2,866,973	D184,204
1921	1,364,063	D56,844	1960	2,919,443	D186,973
1922	1,401,948	D60,121	1961	2,966,681	D189,516
1923	1,440,362	D61,748	1962	3,015,103	D192,004
1924	1,478,996	D63,675	1963	3,070,801	D194,304
1925	1,521,590	D66,346	1964	3,116,487	D197,269
1926	1,568,040	D69,170	1965	3,163,865	D199,955
1927	1,612,700	D71,772	1966	3,226,729	D203,379
1928	1,654,521	D74,159	1967	3,295,143	D206,567
1929	1,696,897	D77,347	1968	3,360,800	D209,732
1930	1,742,181	D80,254	1969	3,419,907	D213,084
1931	1,787,424	D82,966	1970	3,487,470	D216,419
1932	1,839,190	D85,903	1971	3,551,909	D219,637
1933	1,892,663	D88,847	1972	3,631,539	D222,793
1934	1,941,449	D91,258	1973	3,707,729	D225,695
1935	1,985,878	D94,179	1974	3,781,914	D229,729
1936	2,026,516	D98,045	1975	3,858,241	D234,033
1937	2,066,309	D102,601	1976	3,930,271	D238,315
1938	2,104,004	D107,738	1977	4,000,520	D242,881
1939	2,142,080	D112,765	1978	4,065,812	D246,811
1940	2,185,170	D118,358	1979	4,131,952	D250,676
1941	2,227,418	D124,503	1980	4,180,867	D253,796
1942	2,268,540	D130,989	1981	4,242,757	D257,746
1943	2,307,007	D134,717	1982	4,308,622	D262,495
1944	2,338,081	D136,946	1983	4,366,579	D267,440
1945	2,366,154	D139,862	1984	4,423,523	D272,009
1946	2,391,856	D143,386	1985	4,490,855	D276,949
1947	2,413,675	D146,165	1986	4,562,596	D282,020
1948	2,433,824	D148,267	1987	4,633,526	D287,540
1949	2,457,797	D152,235	1988	4,716,594	D293,500
1950	2,492,944	D156,686	1989	4,794,652	D299,180
1951	2,536,016	D161,404	1990	4,890,335	D305,275
1952	2,580,379	D165,568	1991	4,980,927	D313,301
1953	2,624,046	D168,527	1992	5,077,836	D322,878
1954	2,664,562	D171,241	1993	5,175,886	D332,170
1955	2,698,434	D173,777	1994	5,274,846	D342,818

Weights, Measures and Conversions

ABBREVIATIONS

Carat	=ct. or c for gemstone
Karat	= k (for gold)
Troy	= t or no abbreviation
Pound	= lb.
Pennyweight	= dwt.
Ounce	= oz.
Kilogram	= kg.
Gram	= g.
Grain	= gr.
Dram	= dr.
Avoirdupois	= avoir.

METRIC SYSTEM

1 inch	= 25.4 millimeters	
1 millimeter (mm)	= 0.039370 inches	
10 millimeters (mm)	= 1 centimeter	= 0.3937 inches
10 centimeters	= 1 decimeter	= 3.3970 inches
10 decimeters	= 1 meter	= 39.3700 inches

TROY WEIGHT

1 grain (gr.)	= 0.0020833	= 0.0648 grams (g)
24 grains (gr.)	= 1 pennyweight (dwt)	= 1.5551 grams (g)
20 pennyweights	= 1 ounce (lb.t.)	= 31.1035 grams (g)
12 ounces (troy) (t.)	= 0.822857 lb.	= 373.2417 grams (g)
1 pound (troy) (t.)	= 0.822857 lb. avoir.	
1 pound (troy) (t.)	= 1.09714 oz. Avoir.	

CONVERSION FACTORS

Pennyweights to grams:	Pennyweight x 1.552	= grams
Ounces (t.) to grams:	Ounces (t.) x 31.1035	=grams
Grams to Pennyweights:	Grams x 0.06430	= pennyweights
Grams to ounces:	Grams x 0.0322	= ounces (t.)
Avoir. weight to troy weight:	Avoir. weight x 0.832	= troy weight

Bibliography

Andrèn, Erik. Swedish Silver, New York, M. Barrows and Company, Inc., 1950.

Belchem, John and Price, Richard Price. A Dictionary of Nineteenth-Century World History, Oxford, Blackwell Publishers, 1994.

Bernstein, Paul and Robert W. Green. History of Civilization, Volume II: Since 1648, Totowa, Littlefield, Adams and Co, 1971.

Bonney, G. E. The Electro-Platers' Handbook, London, Whittaker and Company, 1905.

Bradbury, Frederick. Bradbury's Book of Hallmarks, Sheffield, Frederick Bradbury Publications, 2002.

Catalogue No. 13, Spring and Summer, 1875, Montgomery Ward and Company, Chicago, 1875.

Catalogue of Baird-North and Company, Salem, 1898.

Catalogue of W. B. Clapp, Young and Company, Chicago, 1878.

Chaffers, William. Hall Marks on Gold and Silver Plate, London, Bickers and Son, 1874 ed.

Davis, Frank. French Silver, 1450-1825, New York, Praeger, 1970.

Dobrotin, Mischa. Metals, Placentia, Amerika Publishing Co., 1993.

Feild, Rachael. MacDonald Guide to Buying Antique Silver and Sheffield Plate, London, MacDonald and Company, Ltd., 1988.

Grandjean, Serge. L'Orfèvrerie du XIXe Siècle en Europe, Paris, Presses Universitaries de France, 1962.

Hartemink, Ralf. "International Civic Heraldry", 1996. URL: http://ngw.com

Hughes, G. Bernard. Small Antique Silverware, New York, Bramhall House, 1957.

Kovel, Ralph and Terry. American Silver Marks, New York, Crown Publishers, Inc. 1989.

Lethaby, W. R. The Artistic Crafts Series of Tehcnical Handbooks, No. II. Silverwork and Jewelry, New York, D. Appelton and Co. 1912.

Link, Eva M. The Book of Silver, New York, Praeger Publishers, 1973.

Markham, Christopher A. Hand Book to French Hall Marks on Gold and Silver Plate, London, Reeves and Turner, 1899.

New Illustrated Catalogue of the Mermod and Jaccard Jewelry Company, Saint Louis, 1889.

Rainwater, Dorothy. American Silver Manufacturers, Hanover, Everybodys Press, 1966.

Streeter, Edwin. Gold: Legal Regulations for the Standard of Gold and Silver Wares in Different Countries of the World, London, Chapman and Hall, 1877.

Swaab, Shirley Sue. All About Silver, 1966.

Tardy. International Hallmarks on Silver Collected by Tardy, 2000.

The Art-Journal Illustrated Catalogue of the Industry of all Nations, London, George Virtue, 1851.

Tariff Act of 1930 [19 U.S.C. 1304 (b), (b)(1)]
  Similar provisions were contained in the preceding tariff acts. Tariff Act, 67th Cong., 2d Sess., Ch. 356 (1922), Tariff Act of 1913, 63rd Cong., 1st Sess., Ch. 16. §F. subsection 1, Act Aug. 5, 1909, 61st Cong., 1st Sess., Ch. 6, Tariff Act of 1901 [33 U.S.C. (Country of origin and quantity of articles to be marked, §8)], Act July 24, 1897, 55th Cong, 1st Sess., Ch. 11, §8, Act Aug. 27, 1894, 53rd Cong, 2d Sess., Ch. 349, §5, and McKinley Tariff Act, Act Oct. 1, 1890, 51st Cong., 1st Sess., Ch. 1244, §6

The Illustrated Catalogue of the Universal Exhibition Published with the Art Journal, London George Virtue, 1867.

True Politeness. Handbook of Etiquette for Ladies, New York, Leavitt and Allen, 1853.

van Dongen, C. B. and G. Nieman. <u>Keurtekens op Zak</u>, Rotterdam, Stichting Belastingmuseum Prof. Dr. Van der Poel, 1998.

Wyler, Seymour. <u>The Book of Old Silver</u>, New York, Crown Publishers, 1937.

The following assay offices provided information for this book:

Assay Office of Hungary at:
  http://www.nemesfemvizsgalo.hu/manevi/index.html

Assay Office of Poland at:
  http://www.gum.gov.pl/pl/site

Assay Office of Portugal at:
  http://www.incm.pt

Assay Office of Russia at:
  http://www.assay.ru

Assay Office of Sweden
  http://www.sp.se/kattfoten/eng/assay.htm

Edelmetaal Waarborg Nederland at:
  http://www.ewnederland.nl

Japan Mint at:
  http://www.mint.go.jp/eng/menu/index_e.html